THE HISTORY OF MY INSANITY

TRISHA PAYTAS

ISBN-10: 1482660067
ISBN-13: 9781482660067

CHAPTER 1

THE BIRTH OF A LEGEND

So maybe "legend" is a bit of a stretch? After all, what exactly have I done in my twenty-four years of existence? I would say I'm working on my plan to waste my entire life, but alas, this is not true either. I want to make something of myself, leave a mark on this world. I've already posed naked, so now it's time to strip back and give you the history of my insanity.

How do these things start? Wow. I haven't read a book since I dropped out of college. No, that's a lie. I read those Fifty Shades books. By the way, this is me writing this, no ghostwriter, no recording device. It's a Friday night, and I'm all alone, so I thought why not just crank out my autobiography tonight? Yes, I'm motivated like that. I digress.

Trisha Kay Paytas was born May 8, 1988, in Riverside, California, to parents Frank Jude and Lenna Kay Paytas. She had a pleasant childhood, a middle-class upbringing with stable parents, and a happy heart until she turned three years old, when her life plummeted…

OK, too morbid? Too self-deprecating? Well, this book is all about Trish, my feelings, and how I perceive things. Should I give away the ending? No. Just keep reading.

My parents divorced when I was three years old. I can't give details because anyone with divorced parents knows there are five hundred sides to every story. My dad will say my mom cheated, and my mom will say my dad refused to move back to Illinois with us; whatever the case may be, I decided to stop caring why really early on. I advise anyone with divorced parents to do the same. It's not worth the fights and getting upset. You will love both your parents, regardless; no point in trying to figure out who was the evil one who broke up the happy home.

So at three years old, my mom moved my brother, Nick, and me back to Illinois, and I have to assume my father was OK with it at the time and moved with us, as there are laws for taking children out of the state, blah blah blah. He said he couldn't find work back there, and so he moved back to California without us. Herein lies the beginning of my abandonment issues. Dad, if you're reading this, I don't blame you—well, at least not anymore. I held grudges against my dad for many years. More on this later. Both my brother and I have been to therapy regarding feeling abandoned by our father, but let's just be clear: our mother was no saint either. I suppose we're all a little hard on our parents, but I'm pretty sure my mental illnesses developed after birth as part of nurture over nature.

Seeing as I can't remember much before five years of age, let's fast-forward. My dad is in California while my brother, mother, and I are in Illinois. Northern Illinois is where my mother had grown up and where her family was at the time. It was at this time my mom met my first stepfather, her third husband and second baby daddy. Are you confused yet? I sure was…am…something. The only good thing I can say about this man is that he gave my family and me our little sister, Kalli. I love Kalli more than anything now, but at the time I remember resenting her. I think I resented her for about eighteen years. Ding, ding, ding! The second theme of this book, English majors, is resentment! One, abandonment issues, and now we have two, resentment. Let's keep going, shall we?

I made faces at her in her crib, and growing up I made her play second fiddle to me. It was also at this time, when I was five, that I remember developing my love for entertaining and acting, or as my mom referred to it, lying. I would make up crazy stories to tell my mom about finding Native American ghosts in our backyard or about me discovering I was a witch and had magical spells. My mom put liquid dish soap in my mouth for every lie I told. I told a lot; my imagination was wild.

I never had any friends all through elementary school. Before I was in the first grade, we had already moved from one hillbilly town to the next. It was hard for me to make friends. Nobody wanted to play with me, so I played by myself. In later years at elementary school, I made up stories about my father because kids made fun of me for not having him around. I would say he was a superrich producer in Los Angeles or a spy or anything that would make them like me. I also said I had a twin sister, Trixie, who lived with him. I would tell kids he had a stage in his house for when I came over, and he'd buy me whatever I wanted, which he actually did.

Neither my father nor my mother was rich for the first half of my life, but they sure made it seem that way. My mom took us shopping and out to eat and to the movies on the weekend, and my dad flew back to see us once a month. When my dad took me shopping, he bought me everything I wanted. My greatest trick was at the toy store. I would say, "Dad, I can't decide if I should get this doll or this doll," and he'd tell me to get both. Oh! Do we have another issue to add to Trisha's list of problems? Why, yes we do—shopping addiction and attachment. It made me happy instantly and fixed any doubts or problems I had with my father. My mom got so furious with all the toys we brought home. She said he was doing it because he felt guilty for leaving me. Hmm, if I make people feel guilty, I get things? Awesome. A wonderful life lesson taught by my mother.

My first stepfather was in and out of our house and his relationship with my mom. I recall my brother, Nick, calling the cops on him for getting physical with my mother. I remember my mother saying awful things about him. Long story short, he had an affair with my mom's sister. I think that was pretty much the end of that.

Cut to Trish, age ten. Enter middle school. Enter Stepdad Number Two, only a few months after the official split from Stepdad Number One. Stepdad Two was a mess. He was old with no teeth. Later in life I asked my mother, why this guy? Her answer about him, as well as all the other men she'd married, was, "Financial reasons." It's a sad truth. I don't judge her. I appreciate her honesty. All sarcasm aside, it did teach me a really important life lesson early on, which was to make my own money and rely on no one else, a concept I understood but couldn't carry out.

This was a time when I thought of my father as the hero. I imagined that one day I would move to California and live the life of a child star with my dad buying me everything I wanted, and I would just live my dreams of performing. Every Easter, summer, and Christmas, I flew to California with Nick, and we lived every child's fantasy every day. We went to amusement parks every week, rode in limousines to look at Christmas lights, ate fast food and doughnuts all the time, and went shopping at toy stores whenever we wanted. My dad spoiled us, but all the while he was working on his start-up company for nineteen hours a day and living off credit cards.

Unlike my mother, my dad was really good at not introducing us to random people he dated. He was very cautious about who he let into our lives. I had met two girlfriends of my dad's since he and my mom split up, and they were pleasant enough, but my attachment to my mom was so strong, I just wanted them to go away. Plus, every child of divorce's fantasy is that their parents will get back together, so having a possible threat come in was *no bueno*. The last one he dated was very nice to us at first, especially me. While my brother and father would go play golf, she'd take me shopping and do girly things. I appreciated this so much 'cause I was superspoiled and did not want to do anything that was not fun for me.

Of course, with each stepparent who came into the picture, keep in mind, each parent was interrogating me for any wrongdoing by the opposite stepparent. The competition to be the better parent, or have an advantage over the other, started very early on.

So Trish is pretty happy, right? I'm getting spoiled with toys, eating all the food I want, whenever I want, and flying to California for vacations three times a year. Sure there are some issues, but my mental health is still pretty intact. I'm not seeing objects that don't exist…not yet.

CHAPTER 2

JUNIOR HIGH HELL

Kids are cruel. Everyone gets bullied, and everyone gets made fun of.
Junior high consisted of three magical years of being tormented as the
insecure Trish. My insecurities began in the sixth grade. Gym class.
We had swimming as part of the curriculum. I remember walking out
in my one-piecer and everyone snorting, making piggy noises. I was so
confused. I wasn't sure why they were doing this. My weight wasn't an
issue in my mind at the time. I was about five feet tall, and I distinctly
remember weighing one hundred pounds even. I didn't think that was
that big. I didn't really grasp the concept of the word "fat" at the time.
I didn't. I was so unsure of the piggy noises, it didn't bother me until
later that week, when this kid, we'll call him "D," asked our homeroom
teacher, "Why is Trish allowed in the classroom? She's too fat, and she
should be with the pigs outside." I remember feeling the sting of this,
as my teacher sort of gasped and paused at what he said and the other
children laughed. I knew it was embarrassing, but again, I didn't understand. Why me? I wasn't the skinniest girl, but I was far from the fattest.
We are talking the Midwest here. I mean, half of the kids in my class
were definitely two times my size.

This went on all through the sixth grade. D and his friends would
say stuff about my rolls, then about my hairy legs and my hairy lip. In
gym class, I was the last one picked. At this point I was still fighting for

acceptance. My mom would take me shopping at Limited Too, where all the popular girls shopped, and my dad even paid for a limo to take me to the lip-synch contest at our Halloween carnival. When word spread my dad was renting me a limousine for the event, a couple of girls agreed to be in my lip-synch group, where I was Britney Spears and they were my backups. It was fun, and I felt like a star because I knew I was a good entertainer. It all felt good until the following Monday at school. Everyone started saying how gross I was in my red latex jumpsuit, and girls in the eighth grade made fun of me on the bus for being a terrible dancer, and most of them just classified me as "too weird to talk to." I think between the limos, my big hair, and my random trips to California, people in this small town were afraid. People fear the unknown, and I was about unknown as they came. No one ever heard of a girl taking off class to go to a book signing in LA or to go to an acting class in Hollywood. I came back from trips with pictures of me on Hollywood Boulevard or swimming in the winter at the beach. It made the parents talk, and in turn, it made the kids talk.

It didn't help either that my relatives lived in the same town. My mom has always had issues with her sisters. I think they were always jealous of my mother. My aunts were heavy, and my mom was always skinny. My mom actually got out of the small town for a while when she married my dad. I think they thought of her as a black sheep, which in turn made my siblings and me black sheep. Of course my cousins caught on to the drama and didn't make things any easier for me at school. For some reason, my brother was always able to make friends pretty easily. I don't know if it was because he was more reserved and didn't push people's buttons the way I did, but I just was never able to make friends.

Seventh grade came and went—new fat jokes, same old kids. Britney Spears had really hit at this time, and she was everything I wanted to be: young, beautiful, blonde, and adored by millions. She was my idol. I loved how she dressed, how she talked, and her makeup. She was like a living, breathing doll. I wanted to be just like her, though I was still trying to fit in, still dressing in Limited Too and going to high school football games.

I think the final straw of wanting to fit in came at the end of my seventh-grade year. Cheerleading tryouts were taking place. I wanted to try out because I wanted to be popular, be like Kelly Kapowski in *Saved by the Bell*, wear the uniform, and have attention on me. I tried out, and I didn't make it. The most mortifying thing wasn't that I didn't make it; it was at school, when all the girls were talking about how fat my legs looked in my spandex shorts. They all wore shorts called Soffes, but I wore spandex because the Soffes rode up on me. It mortified me to the point that I had my dad's friend, who was a doctor, write me a note to get out of gym class for a month. The rest of the year I had to fake injuries or sicknesses to avoid running laps and being seen in shorts.

The summer between my seventh- and eighth-grade years, Nick dropped over fifty pounds and grew about six inches. I didn't lose weight, but I started to find myself that summer in California. I shopped at stores exclusive to California, which gave me a feeling of superiority. That feeling that I was better than what people saw. *I am better than most people because I have dreams, and I'm not going to let anyone tell me I can't achieve them.*

It was during this transition that I declared I wanted to be an entertainer: you will notice me, and you will see I am special. This was also the summer when Stepdad Number Two left and then came back and then left again. Stepdad Number Two was an alcoholic, and I remember being so frightened of coming home and him harming my sister or my mom. He was a violent drunk, and my mom confided in me multiple times that she was scared of him. Stepdad Number Two abused my mom both mentally and physically, and I was constantly worried that something would happen to my girls while I was away. However, when he left the second time that summer, my mom assured me it was for good and that she was not going back to him. I was relieved, and I told her I secretly wished she and my dad would work things out.

When the summer was over, my dad came back a week or so before school started to visit us again, and I remember my mom asking my dad at the front door to work things out. My dad denied her, and it confused me. I'm sure it hurt her. Why wouldn't he try? Why wouldn't he try for us? For the sake of us getting to see him every day? That hurt. He had the opportunity to be with us every day, and he didn't want it. I took it as a personal attack on me, the second strong feeling of being unwanted. My brother later confessed he felt abandoned in a sense, and that my mom finding all these new guys made him feel that he wasn't good enough as the man of the house. For the record, my brother watched my little sister and me all the time. My mom worked three, sometimes four jobs throughout our time growing up. I give my brother a lot of credit for taking care of us. I know he worried a lot about us, and I know his issues add up as high as mine. Pretty sure he's insane as well; he just has a way of masking it better than I do. I love you, Nick.

Eighth grade was upon me. This was the year of sex-bomb Trish. I wore heavy eyeliner, cheetah-print pants, different-colored hair, and my mom's water bras. I wanted attention, and I was going to get it. My mom was back with Stepdad Number Two after my dad's rejection, and my dad had his girlfriend, who was obviously more important than us kids in Illinois. My brother had sports, and my sister had her dad within miles of her. Where was Trish's spot in this world? It wasn't cheerleading or sports. It was performing; it was getting attention. Lies? Perhaps. I told stories of being an extra in movies like *The Big Green* and *Home Alone 2*. I told stories of getting plastic surgery and meeting celebrities. I have to say my knack for meeting my idols always did impress me. The previous summer I had convinced my dad to take me to Las Vegas to meet Donny Osmond—mission accomplished. I had about ten copies of that picture of Donny Osmond and me, and I put them inside my pencil case, in my locker, and on my notebooks. I think the lie I told about how I'd met Donny was that my mom had dated him. I can't really recall, but the truth was my dad splurged for two meet-and-greet passes, just me and my dad.

I tried out for the school play and got the lead role, a character named Dutch. I think the play was called *Sam Spade and the Shrew*. I had all the lines, and even though kids still snickered about the way I looked and dressed, I remember one popular girl, we'll call her "Z," commented at the end of our school performance, "Trish was absolutely amazing." It tickled me so much. People were nice to me when the school play was happening, and they saw me in a different light. I liked the attention. I liked people liking me for doing something impressive.

I also liked the attention my water bras were getting me, not from the boys in my grade, but from my teachers. My male teachers always gave me hugs in the mornings; even my gym teacher hugged me, and I was terrible at gym. I actually started wearing double bras, and pretty soon, I didn't have to do homework. I got extra credit for staying in during recess and helping clean boards and all that fun stuff. Female teachers were a different story. I had one female guidance counselor who literally laughed in my face when I told her I wanted to move to LA to pursue entertainment; she told me that wasn't a job and nobody made money from doing that. You've got to love small-minded America.

Male attention was great, and my teachers were hot. My fantasies went wild about teacher-student affairs. They always fascinated me, and for the first time in my life, men wanted to be around me, wanted me to be with them, and not just for holidays and summer.

Stepdad Number Two had left, and this time he served my mom with divorce papers, so I was getting more attention from my mom, attention from kids and teachers at school, and attention from my dad through his online shopping for me. I remember he had the credit card number memorized when I asked him to order me stuff. I'd be on the phone with him while he was placing the order, and it made me oh so happy. I wasn't "the fat girl" anymore, or "Nick's little sister." I was Trish. I was Trish with the money. Trish with the Hollywood life. Trish with the connections. I also did local pageants, and my mom got me in the local papers by paying fifty bucks or so; in hillbilly land that was famous. I had made it. So life was great, grand, and good, or at least I pretended it was until the holidays.

CHAPTER 3

THE EVIL STEPMOM

Lord help my family forgive me for writing this book. I am not writing this book to hurt anyone. I am almost twenty-five years old, and I promise you I am free and clear of all grudges at this point. I am writing every detail of my life to help someone, anyone, one person going through the same thing, and to remind people that they are not alone, and it does get better. This is a book, after all. What's a book without a happy ending? Maybe. Actually, I can't promise the happy ending, so just keep reading, OK?

Eighth grade, January 2, the day before my brother and I were headed back to Illinois after a long winter break, my father brought me into his bedroom with Nick, and they said they had something to tell me. I shot daggers at my brother for not preparing me for this. Nick and I were always on the same page. Nick was the one person who traveled back and forth with me to California, and we were inseparable. He was the only one I ever felt could understand what I was feeling through our stepdad situations and other hardships.

My dad told me he was getting married…tomorrow.

Shell shock. I hate confrontation or feeling awkward, so I was like, "Yay, I'm so happy for you," when in reality I was livid. My stepmom was OK; she wasn't fun, she only ate healthy foods, and she wasn't very girly, but none of that really mattered at the time. What mattered to me was my dad was getting married, and that meant the door would officially be shut on any chance of him and my mom reuniting. My dad wasn't like my mom. I knew if my dad ever remarried, it would be forever. He'd always told me the only reason for divorce was if (a) someone physically abuses you and puts you in danger; or (b) someone cheats. This was my dad's third marriage. I know his first wife cheated on him, and according to my dad, my mom cheated on him. I always had a theory my dad settled with dear old Stepmommy because she would never cheat because she was plain and just sort of bland. My mom was a knockout, a blonde bombshell, but Stepmommy was quite the opposite.

They got married the next day. My brother and I flew home that night, and we were the ones who had to tell our mom. From what I remember, we didn't tell her for about a month or so. I do remember her asking my dad to get back together again, and when he said he couldn't, that's when we told her he had gotten remarried.

We should've told her right away, but we were hardly teenagers yet. Why was that our responsibility? I think this made my mom angrier than it made us. I think she got back together with Stepdad Number One for a short period at this time. Together they would corner me with questions about whether Stepmommy was abusive. I remember coming back from a London trip with Stepmommy, and my feet were all bloodied. I had blisters from all the walking we did. She was a health nut, so we had to walk everywhere, and I was not wearing comfortable walking shoes. My mom was livid, even more so than the time my dad let me get a perm because I asked for it.

The battle was never-ending between Mom and Dad, from here to eternity. As soon as my dad remarried, the hate spewed from every end. I had to hear from Stepmommy now how terrible my mom was. Dad and Stepmommy would try to lure me out to live in California, which I wanted very badly. I just didn't understand why they wanted me. I thought maybe, just maybe, it was because my dad wanted to spend time with me. Nope.

Here's where the root of all evil comes into play: money. More money, more problems. My dad sold his start-up company for millions of dollars just months after the wedding. I wasn't aware of that at the time. I had to find out about it from—who else?—the kids at school. Some of Nick's friends had found articles about my dad selling the company by typing our last name into searches, which was what everyone did at that time because the Internet was still a fairly new thing. It trickled down to me, and I didn't comprehend it, nor did I understand if it was real. My dad and his wife ended up moving into a mansion; it was huge and beautiful, and it was where I wanted to live. It was in California, where I had started taking acting classes in the summer, and it was where I wanted to be so badly. I didn't think of moving there as a reality until the following winter.

Freshman year got out for winter break, and instead of flying to California to be with our dad for a couple of weeks and then flying back to Illinois, my brother and I drove out to California because my brother was moving into the mansion to start college early. I was so jealous. We drove out in my brother's one-year-old Explorer, which my dad had given him as a sixteenth birthday present. My dad had always asked me what car he was going to get me for my sixteenth birthday. I always said a Volkswagen Beetle, of course. I knew I was getting that as soon as I turned sixteen.

Coming back home alone was a terrible feeling. Stepdad Number Two was back in the picture; we had moved to a new house in the same crappy town, and I felt empty without my brother being there. All I could think about was Nick living it up in California, playing golf every day, eating fast food, and going to college. I wanted it, and I couldn't wait three more years.

My mom, my sister, and I went to visit Nick that spring break. We all fell in love with California. My mom wanted to move out right then and there. She had just lost her father, our grandpa, the year before. But alas, my sister's father, Stepdad Number One, wanted to make our lives miserable and not allow my sister to leave the state, even though he only saw her about once a year—and that was because he made her see him, not because she wanted to.

Even though my mom and sister weren't able to move out, I knew I still had a chance because my dad was out there, and he was asking me to move. My mom knew how badly I wanted to be in LA to pursue acting and be around people who weren't living in a bubble. She also knew my situation at school was not easy; girls were mean, and people were cruel. I was eating lunches alone in the bathroom. My mom supported me and loved me, and she gave me the OK to quit school, move in with my dad, and start school in California. I moved in with my dad and Stepmommy, thinking this was going to be sunshine and red carpets; boy, was I wrong.

My brother had taken over their guesthouse, and I claimed the big room upstairs there. I even had my own bathroom. I started school at the local high school. I lasted four days.

I was not in Kansas anymore. Again, I was a little shell-shocked. My high school in Illinois had about four hundred students; this school had over four thousand. I didn't stand out anymore. I was competing against girls with midriffs showing and kids who drove Mustangs. Girls weren't just thin; they were anorexic. Lies spewed out right away.

My angle this time was that I was a farm girl who'd never been to a real school before. I presented myself as Elly May from the *Beverly Hillbillies*, and that was my character. Nobody cared to get to know me, though. No teachers gave me special attention. I gave up. I cried and put on the waterworks for my dad, saying it was too tough, the classes were too hard for me coming from no-real-education-town USA. My dad let me drop out, and we looked into homeschooling classes so I could finish high school within a year. I started Catholic homeschooling that summer, but I was only interested in my acting classes in LA. I stopped doing my work for homeschooling and focused only on my acting.

It took a couple of months for my dad to catch on that I was failing and not handing in assignments. He wouldn't let me take driving lessons, and he pulled me from acting classes in Los Angeles. Gone were the days of shopping and going out to eat. I had to eat my stepmommy's cooking, which might as well have been poison, and I had to do chores. My mom never made me do chores, but Stepmommy made it clear she was in charge of me now. *Oh really? I don't think so.* I defied her every chance I got; she was truly evil. She got in screaming matches with my brother, and she manipulated the stories she told my dad to make it seem like I was the one with the issues. "Stepmommy" became "my dad's wife," and let me tell you, my dad's wife needs to sit down and write her autobiography, because I really would like to know how she became insane; she is certifiable.

Her lies put my fibs to shame. It was astonishing. I was not doing my work, so my mom felt that was cause for me to move back. In fact, in July of that year she demanded I move back in with her. We talked every day about my issues with my dad's wife, how controlling she was, and how she was deterring my dad from helping me with anything I wanted to do. My mom said, "Move back home and it'll all be better." My boiling point came when my dad and his wife told me that I was never allowed to go to Los Angeles ever again. That put me on tilt, and when my mom told me the real reason why my dad had wanted me out there with him, I knew I had to go home.

Apparently right after my dad sold his company, my mom caught wind and went back to court for more child support. At that time my dad and his wife were in my ear about pursuing my dreams in California. When I finally did go to California to live, my mom obviously dropped the pursuit for more money, but my dad and his wife went after my mom for child support. *What?* I know, right? My mom was working three jobs while my dad's wife was spending five thousand dollars on curtain rods; it was unbelievable to me. The battle only got worse. Not the battle for me—oh no, who cared where Trish ended up? The battle for money and who got to keep it and who got to take it.

I moved back to Illinois, and there was no way I was going back to my old high school after I had declared I was moving to California and never coming back. So I was in limbo for a good six months of doing nothing. I gained about forty pounds; that was fun. It was stress and depression. I was stressed about school. I was depressed about my family situation. I had no direction anymore.

On top of all that, my dad and mom started this year-long court battle that dragged me to court every other month. My mom was making me testify against my dad, and that broke my heart because my dad tried so hard to make me happy even if his wife didn't. I loved my dad. I needed to love my dad for my own sense of feeling sane and normal. My dad called it quits the day I had to go in front of the judge and my dad. My mom made me come to court to testify, and I bawled uncontrollably in the courtroom. I couldn't catch my breath, and at that point, I didn't want to catch my breath. It was only time in my life I would've rather been dead than alive, and that was the lowest point. My dad said, "Stop," before I spoke, and he said, "No more." My dad hasn't taken my side too often in my life, but I will always have so much respect for him stopping that court session so I didn't have to bad-mouth him. My dad saved my life that day, because I didn't want to go on living if I had to choose between Mom and Dad. It was terrible. Parents, please don't ever drag your kids to court; it's traumatizing.

He hugged me and said everything was OK. My mom ended up getting a good chunk of change from my dad. I don't even think it made her happy. I think it made her greedy. This was the turning point of my mom and I being best friends. I resented my mom for making me do that for money. I resented my mom for brainwashing me to move back to Illinois. I resented my mom for cheating on my dad, allegedly.

CHAPTER 4

BACK TO THE FARM

Well, Trish, you're going back to school. Let's try another school. My mom did move us to another small town about a half hour away for me to try another school. I started at an even smaller town that following winter. The high school population was about two hundred—more judgment, fewer teeth, wonderful. However, I did get to create a new character for myself. I was Trish, the girl from Hollywood, of course; my dad was a big-time producer, and my mom was a Playmate. I was a child actor who had moved back to Illinois because my parents had just gone through a fresh divorce. I mean, twelve years is still fresh.

Again, people didn't know how to take me. I started sexing myself up a little more. My mom bleached my hair a brassy blonde. I ripped up my T-shirts and threw birds and crap in my hair and called it fashion. I think with all my razzle-dazzle, people didn't notice my weight. I dropped about thirty pounds, though, by not eating for two weeks straight; that helped. In classes, I volunteered more often to read because these kids were slow—like, all of them. I would read superquickly, and the teachers actually marked me down if I didn't slow down. The kids loved it because they thought I was from another planet, speaking another language; it was sort of my signature at this school. It was my piece of attention. "Who wants to read?" the teacher would ask, and everyone would say, "Trish." I was special. I was better than all of them—score one for Trish.

This school wasn't much different in terms of friends. People still kept their distance here. I was never asked out on dates, nor was I invited to parties. Most teachers loved me except my art teacher; he was a hippie, and he did not appreciate my character. I started really playing up the dumb-blonde card at this school. A show starring Paris Hilton called *The Simple Life* had aired the previous summer, and people did not own televisions in this town, so I knew I could take all the lines from that show and use them as my own. People would talk about Walmart, and I would be like, "Do they sell walls there?" It got people to talk about me; everyone knew Trish. I would say random things like, "Horses don't exist because I've never seen them." Something so outlandish, and they'd believe me. It'd get a rise out of people, and pretty soon we weren't talking about art in the Roman Empire, but we spent an hour talking all about Trish; it was fabulous, and it was attention.

Pretty soon these people began to bore me; school was of no interest, and all I could think about—as I saw Hilary Duff become famous at the age I was at that moment—was that I was wasting valuable time when I should be becoming a star in Hollywood. Hollywood was waiting for me. Hollywood needed Trish, and I was stuck here learning about Future Farmers of America.

This school also showed a lot more physical disapproval of me. I got pencils thrown in my hair, someone threw paint on me, and girls stole my pants after gym class. I always took hate as a sign of jealousy. They clearly wanted something I had, and I loved it, but everyone has her limit of how much she can take. I wanted to quit, and I used the good ol' handy-dandy guilt card on my mom to convince her to let me drop out of school when I turned sixteen. I told her it was her fault I was stuck here, and the least she could do was let me drop out. She actually agreed, but then I got a part in the play. I played Penny Palmer in *Swing Fever*; she was the Marilyn Monroe type who came to a small town and dazzled everyone. I loved playing her, and once again people adored me, and I was the star. So I stayed in school until the end of the year.

I turned sixteen at the end of my sophomore year, and I was ready and waiting for my Volkswagen Beetle to be delivered by my father, as he had done for my brother when he turned sixteen. I waited, waited, and waited, and my dad said I was not getting one. Gee, who was in his ear about this one? My dad had always told me I was getting a car at sixteen, and now that he was a millionaire, he had changed his mind. He was playing the card of "Come to college in California and we'll get you a car here." At this point, I was not holding my breath. This was a huge letdown to me, and it seemed really unfair.

My dad not getting me a car had nothing to do with me and everything to do with my mother and the settlement she got. To this day, my dad won't come out with why he never got me a car, although he got my brother a car. He said he's not allowed to talk about it. Really? Really, Dad, you can't talk about it with your daughter, who has been living on her own since she was eighteen, and you no longer have any ties or connections with my mother? I don't buy it; it's BS, and as far as I was concerned, it was favoritism. What other way is there to look at it?

My dad's wife was always jealous of me; I'm not sure why. Maybe because I was pretty and she wasn't? Maybe because my mom was pretty and she wasn't? Because she never had children of her own? She was always going to be second-best in my dad's life? My dad always made it clear that we were his number-one priority. He always said he would choose us over her, but I don't know if I fully believe that. I always told my dad she was the reason I never wanted to live with him full-time. If my dad had never met his wife, I pictured us living together, even now. I always wanted to live with my dad to get to know him more and make up for lost time as a child, but that was never going to happen with that bit—, I mean, um, woman in the house.

My mom ended up getting me a used car. It was a 1990 Jeep Cherokee, and I loved it. I'd had my heart set on it since we saw *Secret Window* starring Johnny Depp the week before, in which he drove one similar. My license plate even had Depp in the name, but I don't remember it exactly.

My mom told me I'd have to find a job if I quit school. I looked that summer but found nothing, so I went back to school the following fall. I was quite lucky as a teen. I didn't have to work, and my parents gave me spending money as long as I did well in school. I wanted to quit again right away and just move out on my own and become a stripper, but I stayed for one reason and one reason only: my junior-year biology teacher. We'll call him "Mr. D."

He wore glasses, he was buff, he was the football coach, and he was smart. He knew everything about movies, and we'd talk about De Niro and Tarantino all through class while other kids just texted. He let me do science projects on the black mamba and let me use quotes from *Kill Bill* to present it. He was so cool, and he was my outlet. He gave me special attention. I got to go to his classroom during his open period, and he gave me movies to borrow. He loaned me *American Beauty*, and I swore it was a sign. I tried out for cheerleading just so he could see me in the light Kevin Spacey saw Mena Suvari. It wasn't hard making the cheerleading squad at this school. Mr. D never gave me the D—*oh, Trish, that's so crude*—but the fantasy and sexual tension were enough for me. He's the only one I miss from my childhood, and he's the only one I'd ever care to see again. I think he's married with kids. I think he was then, but he was motivation enough to keep me in school and graduate.

Senior year was my living hell. That was when I turned from emotionally unstable to full-on Trish-needs-help. I just wanted to be done with small towns and small-minded people and go out and start auditioning and living my dreams of becoming famous. I mean, being famous meant attention, and that's all I really wanted, just to make money being me. Kim Kardashian beat me to the punch. Damn, if only I were old enough for a sex tape first.

This was the year my mom met her boyfriend from hell. We'll call him "Tiger." Long story, but just think of a famous tiger on a cereal box. My mom started yet another job at a country club about thirty minutes away, and this was where she met Tiger. Tiger started spending the nights in our two-bedroom house immediately. He would get out of the shower in the mornings and walk around our house naked. He sat on my bed naked, and he stole DVDs of mine. My mom never believed me. I mean, I did have a past of lying, but I never lied about Tiger or about any of my stepparents, for that matter. I may like attention, but I'm not going to say someone did something to me when they didn't. I've always been a Catholic and believe in do unto others. Plus I always was aware that karma does come around, so I'm not out to ruin lives. We'd get into really big arguments over Tiger and how I didn't feel comfortable with him in our house. My mom would tell me to get a life, move out, and leave her alone.

She and Tiger would have sex on the couch when I was coming home from football games; she'd have sex in the living room so loudly that my sister and I couldn't sleep, and she didn't care. She stumbled in my room drunk one night, saying she was closing my door so she and Tiger could have loud, crazy sex. She was wearing my Steppenwolf Theatre shirt with no pants, which I later burned. I thought my mom was such a whore, and I thought she was absolutely repulsive.

At the same time I felt trapped. I could not stand to talk to my dad's wife, which meant I wasn't talking to my dad. I had no money to move, and I didn't even know how to go about making money. I had to stay there and endure my mom and her multiple boyfriends coming in and out of the house. I think my mom knew I was flying the coop at the end of that year, so she was looking for her way out as well. We did not get along, and by the end of that year it was safe to say I hated my mom. I resented her and never wanted to speak to her again.

The day I turned eighteen was the second happiest day of my life, and the day I graduated high school was the first. The day of graduation, I ran to get my diploma after the ceremony. My dad was there, and we bolted immediately afterward. I didn't say good-bye to classmates. I didn't say good-bye to teachers. I didn't say good-bye to my mom or sister; they both had made it clear I was unwelcome that entire year, so I just ran. All my boxes were already shipped out to my dad's house, and I was on my way to California; that was the last time I've ever been to Illinois.

CHAPTER 5

COLLEGE DROPOUT

So now you've been reading all about my broken home and thinking, "Trish, you were never molested or beaten, so consider yourself lucky." You may be right; my parents loved me and wanted the best for me, I believe deep down, but my own psyche really was my worst enemy. My peers hated me because I was different, my dad hated me so he left me, my mom hated me so she pushed me out, and my sister hated me because we weren't full-blooded siblings. I just had so many thoughts of people hating me in my head that I didn't feel I deserved to be loved by them, nor did they deserve my love. Anyway, let's get back to the story…

Trish moves to Southern California. Trish enrolls in college that summer. Trish gets a job at Target that summer. Trish looks into acting gigs while attending school full-time. Trish gets Dad's hand-me-down Cadillac, and Dad adds a card on to his American Express package for Trish to use.

I went to community college, which saved my dad a lot of money, considering my brother went for four years to a private Catholic university and Dad's wife was buying properties that never sold. I didn't like where we lived; it was in the middle of the desert. I was working at Target, which was full of depressing employees at the time, and driving a beater. It didn't seem fair that his wife didn't have to work and could just drive around in her Mercedes all day, nor did it seem fair that my brother got to live in a condo on his own his freshman year, while I was living in my dad's guesthouse working my butt off, taking college courses with forty-year-olds and illegal immigrants. My dad would get on my case about buying a dress from Target when I was to only use the card for necessities like toilet paper and shampoo. He demanded I show him the receipts. Well, I'm sure his wife demanded this, because heaven forbid I buy something for myself; that's taking my dad's money out of her pocket for ugly furniture.

I discovered MySpace, and it kept me entertained and took me out of the world I didn't love. I uploaded photos to MySpace, and I became sort of a celebrity on there. All of a sudden I was getting hundreds of picture comments saying how gorgeous I was, and thousands of friend requests were flooding in; this was amazing. I loved it. While most people had an average of about fifty to one hundred friends, I had over fifty thousand within months. The pictures got sexier, and the friends increased. I set up my camera on a tripod and started getting all sorts of naughty. It made me feel good and grown. My dad treated me like such a little kid still. He and his wife would tell me I couldn't wear a certain skirt or not let me go out with friends. So I just put myself out there behind their backs.

I really wanted my fans on MySpace to hear my voice and my personality, and so I found YouTube, the only site at the time where you could record, upload, and share video. I did it strictly for my MySpace fans so they had more ways to dote on me. The first video I ever uploaded was me rapping Vanilla Ice's "Ice Ice Baby." I think I had, like, a couple hundred views, and I was so excited. At the time there were no regular "YouTubers." It was a place for cat videos and babies laughing. Nevertheless, people commented on how funny I was and how the voice and personality weren't what they were expecting. I love that, still to this day. I love shocking people and confusing them in every way.

At Target one day, I was saying how I hated the job but didn't know how to look for a new one. A coworker told me about Craigslist. So I went on one night after school and saw they had a TV and film section.

Jackpot. I was shocked to see people wanting to put people on television. The first ad I replied to was seeking people who were like plastic dolls and dressed over the top. I wrote them the ditziest, most airheaded e-mail you ever read and sent them the link to my MySpace, and they called the next morning right before my class. I skipped class to talk to the casting producer over at *The Greg Behrendt Show*; she interviewed me and asked me if I wanted to be on the show, and I was shocked. It was that easy to get on TV? Yes, of course, I jumped at the opportunity.

She just asked for a family member to go on the show with me, someone in my life who wanted me to "tone down" my look. I talked my brother into doing it with me, and he agreed, but somehow my dad's number got involved. They called my dad and sent him the e-mail I wrote in to the show, and my dad was disappointed in me to say the least. He went over the e-mail with me and asked why I was dumbing down my intellect. I just played my character and said, "Dad, like ohemgeeee, duh, eeeek, that's just the way, like, peeps talk, like gah, get over it."

However, both my dad and brother, I think, took note that it was kind of remarkable I was able to get the attention of a TV show and get paid on top of that. The producers had called both of them and told them they were giving me a makeover to class up my look and that they had a surprise for me. It's quite comical to watch that episode. I think my dad still has it on DVD. I'm wearing pink head to toe, the worst blonde extensions clipped in, and blacked-out eyes, and I talk a mile a minute. Before going out there, I knew I was going to have to make them remember me, and so I talked so fast no one could understand me; the crowd was putty in my hands. I was a born entertainer; what can I say? It was a rush to be on TV, and I didn't care if they were laughing with me or at me; they were laughing, and I was getting noticed.

After the show aired, I got another call from *The Greg Behrendt Show*; they wanted to do a follow-up on my story and let me do a segment for them on Hollywood Boulevard. They were going to follow me around with a camera, and I was going to talk to people with a microphone. I was so excited until my dad's wife had to get involved. I ran into my dad's office, screaming with excitement that they had invited me back for a second TV appearance, and my dad said he had to think about it. Think about it? What? This was my dream. I was getting calls to be on TV. I was going no matter what. Or so I thought.

It was on a school day, which meant I had to take off school, and my dad wasn't keen on that but said as long as I got my work done beforehand, it would be OK. *Great, I'm ready, let's go to Hollywood, Dad.* Nope, hold on. My dad said his wife was going to take me in this time. Why? I didn't like her, she didn't like me, and she was embarrassing. He gave me no reason other than, "She is taking you or you are not going." I cried and pouted, but I had to go. I couldn't say no to television people.

We got there, and I was whisked away to hair and makeup while Dad's wife was left sitting in her car with no access to the lot. When they said I was going to go in a car with them, Dad's wife said she'd come too, and they told her no. How dare they say no to Dad's wife; didn't they know she was Dad's wife? Dad's wife was raging.

As soon as we got home from the shoot, Dad told me no more shoots with *The Greg Behrendt Show*, no more missing class, no more LA trips, ever. Gee, why, Dad? Was it because your wife wasn't included in my opportunity? It wasn't two weeks later, *The Greg Behrendt Show* called me for yet another episode, this time not to talk about my issues but to do a commercial throw for them, as in a real television paid acting job. My dad said absolutely not, and I said, "I'm quitting school and moving out then." I don't think he thought I was serious until I said I found a place and that my mom was coming out to help me move.

Dad and his wife were losing control, and they did everything possible to make my last days there miserable. My dad took away my car and my credit card, and he took away my laptop so I couldn't look for any more jobs, and he took away my cell phone. This was a perfect opportunity for my mom to come back into the picture and make my dad and his wife unhappy, so I knew she'd be in. I will say this about my mom. She had a new boyfriend during this time, and we hadn't talked all summer, not one day since I left my graduation, but as soon as I called her for help, she was there for me.

She came out two days before the taping of my third show, and we packed up my stuff, which was just my clothes, and we headed out to LA to my apartment, which I had never seen. I had just signed the lease via fax. It said it was in the heart of Hollywood, and that was all I cared about. We also bought me a car, a Volkswagen Beetle. This was all thanks to my mom and her friend (not her boyfriend) because I had no money. Never been a saver, always a spender.

I remember leaving my dad's house the way I left my mom at graduation, cold and bitter. He pulled out all the stops to keep me from moving, and he set me up for failure. He had my uncles call me and tell me how many murders took place in Los Angeles every year, but nothing worked. My mind was set, and I was going. My dad's a hard-ass when he doesn't get his way—hmm, like father like daughter.

We got to my apartment right at the corner of Highland and Yucca, just one block from Hollywood and Highland. It was next to a liquor store and an empty parking lot, and needles were all over the grounds. A guy dressed up as Superman, smoking a joint, came to let us in. Welcome to Hollywood. We met with my landlord and moved in my clothes and the air mattress my mom purchased for me on our way up. It was a scary building. I didn't even have locks on my door. It was old and run-down, but I remember feeling so happy and so free. The day we moved in, flowers were delivered. I thought it was some kind of mistake, but it wasn't. The flowers were from Greg Behrendt himself. For those of you who don't know, Greg is the author of the book *He's Just Not That Into You* and was also a writer on *Sex and the City*. I take everything as a sign, and in that moment I knew I was making the right decisions for myself.

My mom stayed and got me situated, and I took her to the taping of the show. It was like a dream. After the show, Greg's sister introduced herself to me and my mother, and we shared stories. Greg's assistant invited us to his house for Thanksgiving, and one of the producers brought us into her office. I loved this producer so much. She really believed in me, and it was great to have someone behind me with no agenda. She gave me paperwork to fill out about this thing called AFTRA, a union that television actors have to join to make sure they get benefits, coverage, and higher pay. It was expensive to join, but my mom loaned me the money, and we did it—best decision I ever made. To this day I get residuals from that show. Now instead of getting a hundred dollars here, a hundred dollars there, I was making scale, a fancy term for a big paycheck for doing a couple of hours' work on television.

The fourth show was the show where Greg told me on camera how much he enjoyed me, how much his staff adored me, and how responsive the audience had been to my appearances; he said he knew I moved to Hollywood on my own to pursue this dream, and he was going to offer me a job, on camera, on his show. If you watched this show, I didn't cry. I didn't do anything because I didn't understand what he meant. I didn't grasp the situation, nor could I believe it. Was it really this easy to just get a job on television?

I worked for the show on and off for the next few months, bringing in big paychecks and working only a few hours a week. I got to make people laugh, perform funny skits, and talk about my feelings; it was the best job ever. I had joined the show midway through season one, and they ended on a show with me on trying to lose weight, to continue in season two. Season two never came; the show was canceled, and they invited me back for the good-bye episode where they had a segment called "The Top Five Trish Moments," which counted down my greatest moments on his show. His assistant brought me flowers. I said good-bye to everyone I had grown to love on that show, and I drove home, sat in a cluttered apartment, and cried and cried and cried.

I didn't save money, my mom ran up her credit card bills on me, and my dad and I weren't speaking. I wasn't going back to college, but I didn't want to go back to working a nine-to-five job either. I tried to live the next few months off of savings, but savings go quickly in Los Angeles, especially when you can't stop spending and can't stop shopping. I met some guys online. I lost my virginity to some random guy and started having casual sex with any guy who would look at me. I never had a boyfriend and never kissed a guy before intercourse. I felt loved because a guy wanted to be with me for a couple of hours. So I went from guy to guy, having sex to feel better about myself and my situation. It didn't help my heart, nor did it help my wallet. I was desperate. I needed money, so I went out and got it, a lot of it.

CHAPTER 6

THE STRIPPER DIARIES

I didn't know what to do, so I went on MySpace looking for answers. I sent out a bulletin asking people how to find jobs, and I got a reply from Alice Cooper. Yes, *the* Alice Cooper. His profile had over one million friends, so I was shocked to see it in my inbox. I must've clicked on the inbox picture a dozen times to verify it was coming from that account before I read it. I opened it while holding my breath. It was from his personal assistant, Brian. Brian said he had seen my picture as he was accepting friend requests, and he thought I was gorgeous. I was flattered, and we began talking. As I felt comfortable talking with him, I asked him if he knew of anyone hiring. He said he didn't but suggested I take up stripping. He told me I was hot enough, which I would've never believed of myself at the time. So I asked him how. He told me he knew the owner at this particular club in Hollywood and that he'd get me an audition.

I went in at the time he said to and met with the owner. The owner was foreign. He looked at my ID and then opened up my shirt and grabbed my boobs. He told me I was OK and that I could start right away. I was intimidated by all the girls dancing. I saw the lap dance room right in the open, and I saw a beautiful, tall, thin, gorgeous girl with big hair and bigger boobs on stage, flipping and dipping, and I was scared. I'd only had sex for the first time months prior, and I had never worn a bikini ever in my life. I didn't have any stripper outfits with me, but the DJ suggested I just go out in what I came in with, which was lingerie under a jean jacket.

Going onstage that night, I was nervous, but I knew I just had to do it. Just do it and get over it, and I was over it almost immediately. Once I was out on that stage bare-ass naked, I thought, "Well, you did it, Trish, the hard part is over." I got guys coming to the stage, and of course girls were laughing at me, but I was getting money.

I was terrible at going up to guys to ask them for dances. Nobody ever told me strategies or what to say. I would talk to a guy for an hour and then chicken out and just leave. I always wanted guys to ask me for a private dance, but that's not how they operate. As soon as I would get up, a girl would come by, chat with the same guy for ten minutes, and get the private dance. I could never figure it out, and therefore I wasn't making nearly as much money as I could have been.

So basically I was living off tips from the stage as my main source of income. I started selling clothes on eBay as well, and then I finally got a slew of part-time jobs on the Boulevard that I just couldn't stand due to dullness. I ended up quitting every job I had within a couple of weeks. I would dance every night but only come home with about fifty bucks. My neighbor was the guy who dresses up as Superman on Hollywood Boulevard. We started talking, and he convinced me to try going out with him on the Boulevard dressed up as Supergirl to make extra cash. I didn't want to at first, but he said *Jimmy Kimmel Live* came out all the time and used him for TV sketches and paid union rates. So I went out, and I actually got to be on one episode of *Jimmy Kimmel Live*, and it was all worth it. I was racking up the TV credits. I felt good. I was exhausted from dancing five hours a night and standing on the Boulevard for eight hours a day, every day, but you always hear, "If it were easy, everyone would be doing it," and it was a heck of a lot better than going to school, living with my dad and his naz—, I mean, wife.

Brian finally asked me out on a date one night, and I agreed. Nobody had taken me out on a date; he was my first. I was almost nineteen, and I was going on my first date. The guys I was having sex with never took me out; they just invited me over to their houses to "hang out" around midnight on occasion. I didn't even know what Brian looked like; all I knew was he had been Alice Cooper's personal assistant for, like, twenty years.

To this day, Brian was my favorite first date. He picked me up, brought me flowers, and had little bags full of gifts for me to open at dinner. He took me to the Grove, but it was too crowded so we ended up eating at a place called Hamburger Hamlet in the Valley. It was awkward to be out with him. He was in his late forties but looked a lot older, slightly balding, bleached hair, and not a handsome face, but I did find him endearing. I opened my gifts at dinner, and they were a bunch of Alice Cooper memorabilia like CDs, DVDs, and even a used makeup towel from the tour.

I found Brian fascinating because of all he had done in his life, how he had gotten the job with AC, and all the other Hollywood adventures he had experienced. I've always had an attraction to older guys. Daddy issues? Perhaps, but I've never dated, nor have I slept with, a guy under thirty years of age. Heck, I've only slept with one guy in his thirties. Everyone else was older. I always say you have to be over forty to ride this ride. OK, like I need to be any more perverted. You get it. Nevertheless, I liked Brian as a friend, but I wasn't sexually attracted to him. Besides, he went to strip clubs, and that just was a turnoff for me. I did go back to his apartment out of politeness; being overly polite is a bad habit of mine. I can't say no to people. We picked up ice cream and went back to his place. We ate it on his couch, and out of nowhere, he looked at the clock, said, "It's midnight, now I'm going to kiss you," and he did; he kissed me with a scoop of mint chocolate chip in his mouth and transferred it to mine. It was cold and unromantic, but I did give him a good minute of make-out time. He tried to go further, but I told him I was celibate, which was a lie—recurring theme, English majors. He stopped, and he said he understood and then drove me home. I didn't think I'd hear from him again, and I was OK with that.

Ladies, a word of caution: if you're meeting someone off the Internet in person, make sure you see a picture of him first, don't let him pick you up at your house, and meet him in public. I was lucky Brian was not a stalker but not so lucky with others; this would be foreshadowing, so highlight that for your thesis.

Brian actually did call me the next day, to my surprise, and he actually asked me out on a second date. This was a new concept to me: don't have sex right away, and they may actually want to get to know you—what a novel idea. He wanted to go out that night, but I had to work at the club, and that was the truth. He showed up that night at the club and was my first lap dance customer. The owner was shocked, as were the girls. I never got dances, especially not within a minute of saying hello. This gesture was actually so sweet of Brian. I know many of you may be like, "Trish, this was just his way to get you naked," but he had known about my struggles with stripping and how it didn't come easily to me. He was very sweet and respectful and kept his hands at his sides. As soon as he left, the owner fired me.

I was confused. I had just gotten a dance. "That's the problem," he said. "You've only gotten one dance the month you've worked here, and it was from your boyfriend, so get your stuff and leave." The one income I really needed just to make ends meet, and I was fired. I called Brian to pick me up, but he didn't answer. A customer from the club followed me outside and heard my phone conversation, and he offered me a ride home. I didn't think anything of it except I needed a ride, and it felt safer than the bus, so I accepted. Side note: I smashed my little Beetle Bug my third day living in LA by hitting a parked car in my complex's parking lot. It was a hit and run by me, but it wasn't hard to track me down. My locks never worked, and my car never ran so well after that, so I used it sparingly.

Here is the part where I'm swallowing spit and rubbing my eyes and wondering if I need to put this in the book. I like to sugarcoat things, but I want to let these feelings, emotions, and experiences out so I don't have to hold them in anymore, so I'm just going to do this and say this in hopes that I can genuinely help even just one person not go through this.

This guy drove me past my house and up, looking over LA. I was a little scared because this was not wanted nor was it even offered. He told me I looked scared and to relax and that he was going to take me home. It was a Lifetime movie come to life. I've watched way too many Hollywood stories about aspiring actresses being murdered because they were floozies or what have you. I really thought this was my punishment for stripping. I remember praying to God that I'd stay alive and that if I didn't to forgive me of all my sins.

As my eyes closed, I felt a hand go up my skirt, and I heard his seat belt come off and his zipper go down. A car went by, and he stopped for a minute and then climbed over the console and on top of me. I didn't cry. I simply asked if he wouldn't. He wasn't violent, and he didn't hit me, but he did tell me to stop talking. I was so fearful he was going to kill me that I stopped talking. As soon as he started having sex with me, I kept saying no. He put his hand over my mouth, and I blacked out. I didn't pass out; I blacked out. I'm not sure of anything that happened next. All I remember is a car pulled up right behind us and turned off its lights, and the guy who was on top of me quickly got off me, started the car, and sped off. I don't know who was in the car or if he knew, I just thought the worst, and it has made me paranoid of being in parked cars ever since. I will not sit in a parked car for longer than five seconds without freaking out.

He did drive me home, and he asked me if I enjoyed it. I said yes at that point to just get away from him. I never saw him again, but I felt so violated, I was shaking for days after. I've never told this story until now. I've hinted to my mom that I've been raped but never come out with the details. It's not as horrifying writing it out, but it still makes me shake; my heartbeat is going faster, and I'm looking around my apartment to make sure the doors are locked.

I was pretty numb after this. I told Brian I was fired, and that's all I told him. He told me there were plenty of other strip clubs, and he was right. I started at another one down the street shortly afterward. Something changed in me that night I was violated. I was numb to men. I wasn't intimidated by them anymore. I started going up to guys and playing on their emotions like I used to with my parents. I would find something to make them feel guilty, tell them lies. I used to say I had children at home. I told them I was a virgin. I said I had a boyfriend who beat me. Pretty soon these guys felt sorry for me and couldn't say no to dances from me.

I was only getting to work one night a week at this club because of all the girls who wanted to work, so I started working at a second club in Van Nuys. This was a ghetto club, all ethnic girls. I was the only white girl working there. I always dressed in baggy and ugly clothes so they wouldn't steal anything from me. I never drove my car because I wanted them to think I had nothing, like them, so they wouldn't feel intimidated by me. I know they were though.

Dances at this club were as easy as standing in view of a guy, and he'd come up and take me by the waist to go pay for me in the private VIP area. These guys weren't like the guys at the Hollywood clubs; these were your illegal construction workers who didn't know any English, spending their entire paychecks on you and trying to cop feels whenever they could. Giving a lap dance to these guys was like being in a wrestling match; you had to keep pulling away and hitting their arms away from you. Guys would stick their nasty-ass fingers in places that made me cry. I hated myself after working these shifts, but it was easy money, and pretty soon, I just didn't care anymore. I drank in the back and blacked out during the dances.

I couldn't take it day after day. I never took drugs, never wanted to. I have such an addictive personality, I'm scared I'd get addicted and couldn't stop. I can't stop searching for love, can't stop eating, can't stop shopping, and for a while I couldn't stop having sex. I just knew I needed more days at the Hollywood club. I couldn't get more days, but a girl who went by the name Exxxotica took a liking to me. She mentioned she had a side business where she hired girls to go to guys' houses for private dances, and they made three times what we made at the club. It sounded enticing. She told me it wasn't dancing we'd be doing, and I immediately got scared and backed out. I may be a dancer, but I am not a prostitute. I said no thank you, went home, and cried.

I got on my knees and prayed, day in and day out, while working at the clubs and on the Boulevard. I prayed to find another acting job.

I even went to church again. My dad took us every Sunday, but my mom never got into the habit. Not two hours after morning mass, I got a call from the producer I worked with at *The Greg Behrendt Show*.

"Trish, I'm working on a new show, and I want you on it. It'll air on Sci-Fi, and it's with Stan Lee. Are you interested?" I didn't know who Stan Lee was at the time, but you bet your bottom dollar I researched him up and pretended to know. The producer got me a fast pass to audition, meaning I auditioned straight for producers. My producer helped me create a superhero for the show *Who Wants to Be a Superhero?* (season two), and we came up with a great character who got her powers from movies and television: her name was Epic. Epic had white hair like Storm from X-Men and a hot little black ice-skating outfit that I used as stripper wear. I took my stripper boots and strutted my little plump thighs in front of Stan Lee at the callbacks. I improved the whole audition, turned up the bubbly, dialed up the dumb, and like magic, I was cast on the show one week later. I quit all my strip clubs, and I said never again. Trish will never be a stripper again. I packed my bags and moved into the superhero house and the reality TV world.

CHAPTER 7

REALITY TV STAR

I still was about a month shy of turning nineteen when I entered the superhero house. I had diagnosed myself as mildly insane, yet somehow I passed the psych test. I lasted three episodes, which was more than I was betting on. It was a fun experience, and even though the show wasn't for me, I did realize I had a knack for being a character. So I started bringing Trish, the reality TV star, with me in the real world, to job interviews, relationships, etc.

During my time on the show, I realized adults are no different from kids in high school; they like to mock what they fear, and they fear the unusual. On the show there was a contestant who condemned me and thought it was his right to judge me. He called me dumb and fake, and it took me a little aback, as I had never had this experience with adults since moving to Los Angeles. I felt like I was in the twilight zone and back in high school with such childish and hurtful actions. His digs at me were captured on camera; he made me cry, and it eventually led to his demise on the show even before mine. In some way, I was numb to it. I cried because I was being humiliated on national TV, but it didn't sting. I guess I was so used to the name-calling from ten years of it as a child and teenager.

I was only in the house for about ten days total, but when I got out, I had a renewed sense of motivation to keep going and keep striving toward my goals in Hollywood. I always give myself the hardest kick in the butt after failure or after someone tells me I can't do something. Being on *Superhero* gave me a renewed self-confidence that I was going to be back on television, that perhaps this may be my break.

Upon leaving the house, I went back to stripping, but I also got a job at a T-shirt shop at the Hollywood and Highland mall. It was fun because I got to design T-shirts for tourists, and I also got to meet celebrities and watch shows being filmed at the Kodak Theater. I felt like I was a part of Hollywood, the business, even if I was just in Hollywood, the ghetto city of Los Angeles.

The club I went to was a new one, a famous one mentioned in Mötley Crüe songs, off the Sunset Strip. I liked this one the best because once again I got to meet celebrities, and I felt like those were my connections. I mean, you always hear about wannabe actresses sleeping with directors and actors and thus catapulting their careers, right? Wrong. I would sleep with any guy I'd recognize from any show; it made me feel special, and I was getting paid. Did that throw you? It threw me too. After I had sex with these guys, they would tip me a couple hundred dollars. When they asked me to come to their houses for sex, I made thousands. A couple thousand dollars may not seem like a lot for sex, and why would these Hollywood hotshots have to pay for sex? They don't; they pay you to leave. None of these actors ever took me out on a date.

My Rolodex of celebrities would put Heidi Fleiss to shame. However, I didn't consider what I was doing illegal. I was willing to have sex with them for free; they just were being overly generous with gas money. Either way I wasn't complaining. I guess I was used to guys not wanting to be around me. If my own father didn't want to live with me while I grew up, why should these random men bother spending any time with me? Again, I felt special that I was sleeping with extraordinary people, when in fact, all it got me was a string of heartaches, depression, and diseases. I would say 90 percent of the actors you watch on television or see in the movies have sexually transmitted diseases; they either don't know, don't tell you, or don't care. I think everyone assumes everyone in LA has something, so no one bothers mentioning it. I actually never got tested for years, for fear of having something. Which is so dumb, but that's Los Angeles girls.

I also continued seeing Brian; he was steady, and he gave me the attention these celebrities weren't giving me. He'd take me out to eat, but after a dozen dates and me not putting out, he started backing off. I think he felt I wasn't attracted to him. We e-mailed every day, but the dates become more and more sparse. Looking back at this time in my life, he really was the best guy for me. I was just too blinded by Mr. Director and Mr. Movie-of-the-Week Guy to actually consider a somewhat normal guy like Brian.

Brian would always end our e-mail conversations with "Ur fuct." I would reply, "No ur fuct," and he would reply, "We both are." I never really fully understood what that meant. I just thought it was something playful.

As I started making money and worrying less about how I was going to pay bills, I noticed my mental positivity was also changing. Maybe it was because I was shopping more. I spent all the money I made from the guys at the club on dresses and toys and cameras and shoes. To this day, I'm such a clothes hoarder. I keep all my clothes because I have such an emotional attachment to them. I still have tags on over 75 percent of my closet. I love my clothes, and they've been with me through it all. I blew through money so quickly, leaving none in savings, that by the time the end of the month rolled around I'd be on the phone with my mom and her friend in Illinois, asking them to send me money, and they would.

I definitely wasn't speaking with my dad at all during this time. As far as I was concerned, my dad was the reason I was raped, my dad was the reason I was stripping, and my dad was the reason I couldn't hold a relationship together. Of course, as I write this, I understand he wasn't the reason. I made those choices, but you do have to wonder, did I make these choices because I was born with something a little off in my mind or because of the way I was raised? That's the age-old question, nature versus nurture. I suppose it doesn't really matter now, but I do think about it, as I don't want to make the same mistakes with parenting when

I have children, if you can call them mistakes. I wasn't perfect, yet I expected my parents to be—makes total sense.

As my mind became a little more positive about being able to survive in LA, I started booking more TV roles. I had small parts on reality shows here and there, and I started doing the talk show circuits; talk shows were the ones that were primarily casting on Craigslist. I had no idea how to go about getting an agent or manager. I still don't. To this day, I've worked over one hundred TV shows, and I've never had an agent or manager. I booked all of those myself. If this book is sounding a little bitter, maybe it's because I am. I've been on my own a lot, whether that was by choice or by force; either way that's the case of my life. I've always made my own opportunities and my own way in this world. No one gave me handouts. I may have gotten breaks, but that was only because I was putting myself in those situations. Even writing this book, I have no publisher. I have no one who showed interest in it, but it's something I wanted to do so I'm doing it. If one person buys this, I will be happy because someone cares about me and my story. If no one buys it, it's been the best therapy money could never buy.

Superhero aired the summer after filming. I had spent my nineteenth birthday alone in my apartment, blogging on MySpace, taking sexy photos and making YouTube videos. If you go to my YouTube channel, and go to my video from May 8, 2007, you'll see nineteen-year-old me dressed as Mr. Blonde from *Reservoir Dogs* dancing to "Stuck in the Middle with You." That was my nineteenth birthday. If you do happen to find the video, you'll also notice my dining room with no table or chairs, just a huge pile of clothes on the floor behind me.

It should also be noted that though I started my YouTube channel for my MySpace admirers to admire me more, it turned into a shrine and tribute to Quentin Tarantino at this time. Quentin's movies were my inspiration for wanting to act and move to LA. For my seventeenth birthday, my mom had taken my sister and me to see *Kill Bill: Vol. 2*, and I remember looking at Uma Thurman and just being in awe of her talent, beauty, and overall ability to kick ass. Not only did I love the setting of films like *Pulp Fiction* and *Jackie Brown*, but I also envisioned moving to LA, meeting Quentin Tarantino, and him asking me to marry him on the spot. We'd live happily ever after in his mansion, and I would star in all of his films.

Well, not to my surprise, I actually did get to meet Quentin right around this time. Remember earlier when I mentioned that if I want to meet someone, I will find a way? I owe this one to director Eli Roth. I mention their names because they were the only positive people I encountered in the Hollywood world, for the most part. They weren't sleazebags, at least not in my experience.

I, along with one hundred thousand other people, was friends with Eli on MySpace. What was cool about his page, as opposed to other celebrity pages, was that he actually blogged and responded to fans. I know I e-mailed him a couple of times via MySpace, and the first time he left a comment on a photo of mine, I remember I panicked. I was getting attention from someone of importance, and it wasn't because I was having sex with him. I had never even met him. I guess he took notice of my admiration for Quentin Tarantino; my name was Grindhouse Barbie on MySpace, my entire background was QT's face, and every video on my page was me acting out scenes from Quentin's movies or reciting monologues performed by Quentin himself.

One day I actually got a private message back from Eli telling me about a special screening of some movie at the New Beverly Cinema down the street from me, and he hinted that Quentin was going to be there. I immediately jumped on that and was the first in line for that screening. I went by myself, as I did most places when I was living in Hollywood, but I distinctly remember Eli and his brother coming up to me; they recognized me from MySpace. Eli asked if I had met Quentin yet. I said no, and he took my hand and led me to Quentin.

Did I mention the recurring theme of me blacking out in this book yet? Maybe one or two times? Well these blackouts happen a lot to me; it's like I go out of my body and can't remember events taking place. After being introduced to Quentin, I remember him asking me if I was the girl who stood out on Hollywood Boulevard as Wonder Woman (Supergirl, but close enough). Then he said something about me doing

YouTube videos, and that's all I remember. I do remember a guy came and took a photo of the three of us, which I thought was cool because I didn't ask for one, and I don't think anyone did because it's not cool to ask for photos with celebrities. Some photographer took the photo, gave me his card, and said he'd send it to me. He never did, but it was OK. I met Quentin a few more times at book signings and stuff, and he always remembered me—and, of course, it was more than appropriate to get photos at those types of events.

If you're still on my YouTube page, look up "Hi to Quentin Tarantino." It's me on *The Price Is Right* spinning the big wheel. Drew Carrey asked me who I wanted to say hi to as it was spinning, and I said, "Hi to Quentin Tarantino," hoping he'd be reminded how beautiful I was and that he'd call me up and ask me to marry him. Never happened. To this day, Quentin is my only idol that I've met who didn't disappoint me. He was always gracious to me and gave me hugs, and it just felt nice to be treated well by any guy, much less by a guy I looked up to. I'm still a huge fan of him to this day.

I think meeting Quentin was the first time I got a sense of the power of YouTube. If I had never made those videos about Quentin, Eli would've never seen them, and I wouldn't have had the opportunity to meet my biggest hero. It was kind of surreal but exciting. Who else could be watching my videos? What else could become of them?

I have to say one more side note on Eli Roth and the MySpace days. I also owe Eli the biggest thank-you for my best friend in the whole world, Jeff. Jeff had cowritten the faux trailer *Thanksgiving* with Eli, and it was featured in Quentin Tarantino and Robert Rodriguez's *Grindhouse*, so obviously I friended Jeff via MySpace after seeing him on Eli's top friends. Jeff is the one and only constant friend I've had in my life. He knew what a crazy stalker fan I was of the trailer, the movie, and of QT, but he embraced my crazy from early on. We talked for years online and then on the phone before we actually met in person, but even now, we talk almost every day. He's my best friend and biggest supporter, and he's been with me through pretty much the rest of this book. He knows all my secrets, and he's never judged. Jeff, I love you so much. I'm so happy my crazy ass stalked you and your friends on MySpace because we are truly two peas in a very messed-up pod. Thank you for loving me unconditionally throughout these past six years. For the record, Jeff and I are really just friends. We've never had sex, and we haven't even kissed, but he has agreed to impregnate me if I'm not knocked up by the time I'm thirty. It's a joke, but one never knows.

Where was I? Oh yes, *Superhero* aired that summer of 2007. I didn't get my big break, but my comic book posters of Ms. Limelight—the character name had to be changed from Epic due to copyright issues—were all over Los Angeles. It was pretty exciting to be on a television show that had posters hanging on walls in Silver Lake and aired commercials during prime time. *Superhero* also brought me a new adventure, which I would be on for the next three years: working the comic book convention circuits all across America.

Most of you have probably heard of the San Diego Comic-Con and think it's a bunch of nerds dressed in costumes once a year, and that's pretty much all there is to it. I know I thought that before I went on a series of comic con tours. In fall of 2007, I spent my weekdays at the strip club and weekends flying across the country to attend comic book conventions with my fellow superheroes. It was pretty exciting to be flown in and stay at a paid hotel and get to meet stars of the past. For those of you who've never been to a comic con or any comic con outside of the San Diego one, let me just give you a brief overview of what takes place at this kind of event in Nowheresville, Midwest, USA.

Comic book conventions take place at a convention center or hotel ballroom, and "celebrities" (i.e., people who might've been on TV back in the 1970s) sell their photos and their souls for twenty bucks. There are also vendors who sell merch, comic book artists who sell their literature, food, costume contests, and a whole lot of locals who put on their best Halloween costumes and parade around in a room full of people just like them. I would say it's a place for nerds to go and not be judged, but after years and years and years of working these shows, I know firsthand, nerds are the most judgmental. If the metal isn't perfect on your slave Leia costume or you don't know what a stormtrooper is (as was the case with me; FYI, they are the ones in *Star Wars* who look like white robots), they laugh at you; literally, they laugh at you—crazy, right?

I was getting booked through this guy who had approached all of us in the *Superhero* cast after the show had aired. He had a bunch of D-list actors, and I thought, well, why not? What do I have to lose? These conventions were solely about money for me at the time. I sold my Limelight headshots for ten dollars and maybe made an extra five hundred a weekend. My booking agent took 10 percent, so it was a little less than that, plus I had to pay for food and for my costume to get cleaned. Around this time I started bleaching my hair bright blonde, so that was always an added expense when I went out of town.

Over the years the comic cons really became more about the experience of meeting people who knew who I was and who wanted to meet me. However, mixed with my "following" were people who wanted something from me. This was the beginning stage of my paranoia. I think once I felt the pressure of being in the public eye, even in a very minor way, it messed with my psyche, my sanity, if you will. Of course sleeping with any guy who looked at me and lived in anything but an apartment really didn't help my mental state either, but I didn't understand that until many years later after many therapy sessions. I'm jumping ahead of myself; we'll get there—we will, right? You're going to keep reading, won't you?

I noticed my fans were mostly middle-aged men, which kind of surprised me. I thought I came across as very wholesome at the time we taped the show, and even at these conventions, my Limelight costume was tame in comparison to all the girls rocking around with pasties and no pants. However, it was cool to have any fans at all. Even to this day, I don't really consider myself as someone who has fans. I like to refer to people who follow my life and career, whether it's on television or the Internet, as supporters, because really, up to the point of me writing this book, what have I really done to earn fans except live my life? Either way I am grateful to you—yes, you—because you are reading my life story, which says you care about my life, hopefully in a positive way, but either way, you care about what I do, and that's all I've ever really wanted in life—for someone somewhere to care about me.

After a full eight hours of signing, we'd go back to the hotels. I was only nineteen, so I wasn't old enough to go to bars, but I'd always follow up with the stars who gave me their numbers. That's another thing you should know about these more random comic cons: they are big orgies. Yes, this is true. I was invited to some fan orgies, where people who bought tickets to the con would gather together in a room for sex, but I've always been a one-on-one sex kind of girl, so I never partook.

If you're a pretty girl (or in some cases just a girl with a vagina), a lot of times these D-list stars would invite you to their hotel room for a bit of an ego boost. Let's face it, if you are a celebrity with actual acting credits under your belt, it must be a bruise to your ego to have to go around and sell your autographs. Do you think Johnny Depp asks people for a twenty-dollar bill when they see him on the streets? No. So my theory with the D-list stars (and I use this term lovingly, as I've dated too many to name) is that they want to relive a little bit of their heyday by scoring all these comic con chicks. I don't say this in judgment. I say this in observation.

I started being one actor's "constant" at each convention we'd go to. He was an actor on a big show in the early 1980s, and he showed up to these conventions with a motorcycle from the series and took pictures with all the ladies sitting on it. He was suave and charming. I met him at nineteen and began a sexual relationship with him at the second convention I attended. To this day, I still get invited to conventions, and I always look to see if his name is on the list. I'm pretty sure he has since retired from the circuit as well, but he still gives me butterflies. He was buff, and he was a star to me. I bought all the DVDs from his show off Amazon, and I'd watch them on my downtime. Every convention we worked together, I grew more and more attached to him and more and more attracted to him. I researched him as well as his show, and I did find out he was married with children, yet I continued to sleep with him.

I'm not really sure why, but I do feel that between this and being an escort to married men, it has brought on a lot of bad relationship karma for me. It's perhaps the only thing I've regretted in my life. It broke my heart knowing that guys were such scumbags, but the fact that I was a part of their scumbag schemes did not make me feel good. The fact is that it was never about needing sex; it was about someone wanting me, choosing me, and loving me. I thought I was so special to have been chosen by a guy when there were hundreds of other girls he could be spending his time with. (And who is to say he wasn't?) I don't justify sleeping with him unprotected, but if a guy told me he didn't want to use a condom after I asked, I said OK. It's such a dumb thing to do. So I take back what I said earlier: I regret two things in my life. Sleeping with married men and sex without a condom—both end in heartache and sickness.

I actually was only on the comic con circuits for a few months before I started wearing down. I was traveling every weekend, stripping every weekday, and having sex through it all, multiple times a day with multiple partners. I wasn't paying my bills because I didn't want to spend my hard-earned money on that. Nineteen-year-old Trish thought she didn't have to pay bills. I blew through all my earned money, not on rent but on clothes, shoes, makeup, and purses. I hardly ate. Sometimes when I look back at the YouTube videos I was putting out at this time, I read the comments, and people say, "Wow, Trish was so skinny, what happened?" I've bettered myself since then; that's what happened. Eventually I got to the point of just not eating because I didn't want to spend money on food. I only ate when I had a date with someone.

I also had cut off ties with pretty much all of my family. I held resentment toward my brother and father for not helping me or supporting me in my move to Hollywood the previous year, and my mom had remarried yet again, this time to Stepdad Number Three, and my sister was busy with her own school life. I really had no support system, mostly because I was too proud to reach out. Then, in December of that year, I had to quit dancing because I had no energy to stand. I couldn't even get up to go to the bathroom. I literally would pee on my futon. The night when I couldn't even get up on my own was the night I picked up the phone, called my dad, and asked him to rush me to the hospital.

CHAPTER 8

FAILING HOLLYWOOD

My dad picked me up at midnight when I called, no questions asked. He helped me to the backseat of the car, where I lay down. I remember being in so much pain; this was the first time I felt so close to death. I remember praying for the first time in a long time, just asking God to forgive me. Whether I lived or died, I wanted God to know this was not the life I thought I'd be living. I didn't understand how I had spiraled out of control, but I put the blame on anyone but myself. I blamed my dad for not helping me out. I blamed the men who'd slept with me and then left me. I blamed my mom for not showing me how relationships worked. In fact, I had made the choices on my own, and I thought I knew everything. I never regretted my first move to Hollywood because I wanted to be on TV, and my dad wasn't going to let me do it. Sometimes you only get one opportunity in life to make your dreams come true…but then again, sometimes you get a dozen.

We got to the hospital—the same hospital I was born in, ironically. My dad still paid for my medical insurance, which I was thankful for. I couldn't even sit up for the nurses to take my blood. They admitted me into a room for the night. It was my first night staying over in a hospital, and the first night I ever used a bedpan. The next morning my dad came back to stay with me. I slept for about three days straight. Nurses and doctors came in, but I had no idea what they were doing or what they were saying. I still couldn't eat anything, but I was hooked up to a bunch of machines that I guess were feeding me in some way. I couldn't stand to shower, nor could I even talk.

Luckily on the fifth day I was able to stand and go to the bathroom and finally able to see clearly. I felt a lot better. The problem was dehydration combined with viral hepatitis. I know the dehydration was the result of me not buying any groceries for myself. I wasn't drinking any liquids except maybe a Coke I would pick up at the liquor store once a day. Viral hepatitis is an inflammation of the liver. I remember I had an abnormal liver count, and I couldn't be released until it was back to normal.

I ordered my only meal I ever ate at the hospital, and it was chicken fingers. They were the best chicken fingers I've ever eaten. I am a chicken finger connoisseur. I've been eating chicken fingers all twenty-four years of my life, and I still dream about those Riverside Hospital chicken fingers.

I was released that fifth day, and my dad came to pick me up. I stayed with him for a few days because I still needed to get better, and to be honest, I needed a break from my dirty apartment and my dirty job and dirty men. Unlike hepatitis B or hepatitis C, viral hepatitis is not a chronic disease. It can be a result of multiple things: food contamination, oral sex, or anal activity. It can also be brought on if you live in a nursing home, travel internationally, or work in health care or sewage occupations, as it's a feces-carried disease. I felt like I needed something clean.

Living with my dad for those few days was so nice. I had all the liquids I wanted and all the medications I needed, and it was warm, and it was clean, and it was familiar. I just watched TV all day and didn't have to worry if I was going to be making money and how much. After staying there and talking with my dad, I told him I was behind in my bills, in a great deal of credit card debt, and I had no job (I wasn't going to tell my dad I was basically a hooker). My dad asked if I wanted to move back and go back to school.

Did I want to? Absolutely not. I was very hesitant about the whole thing. The biggest incentive was my dad offered to not only pay for my school as he had in the past, but also to pay me to go to school. For every class I was enrolled in, he'd pay me one hundred dollars each month. I would have to give him reports on how I was doing, but it sounded like a good opportunity, plus an additional hundred dollars for every A grade I'd get at the end of the semester. I had always been good in school, even if I hadn't liked it, so I agreed. Also, I was on the verge of eviction, and creditors wouldn't leave my phone alone. I thought, what better way to solve my problems than to just escape them? Oh, the intelligence of nineteen-year-olds—they know everything, don't they?

I was paying month to month on my apartment after my one-year lease was up, so it wasn't too big of a deal to move. My dad and brother went up to my apartment with a moving truck and just threw everything into garbage bags. I only had a futon for furniture, so they just tossed that. It was the easiest move I've ever been through. It was a relief to be back at my dad's house. I didn't stay in the guesthouse because his wife had cats up there, so I reclaimed my old bedroom I'd had when I came out for the summers. My dad bought me a real bed with a real mattress. It wasn't sleeping on the floor, it wasn't my blow-up mattress, and it wasn't a futon; it was the best thing that had ever happened to me. Young adults starting out and living on your own: purchase a bed with a box spring and mattress. It's the one thing I would've invested in had I known. It will change your life. It makes any stressful day not stressful. We also refurnished my room with a desk for doing homework and a new flat screen. It felt nice to know I wouldn't have to worry about bills and would get paid to go to school.

I enrolled in classes the winter of 2008 at the same local community college I had started at two years prior. I was going part-time so I would not be overwhelmed. I took an English class and a math class and an online Western civ class. I made it through my first semester pretty easily, but I was getting restless. I missed going on auditions, and I missed dating. My dad made me a deal: if I kept up with my college, I could drive in to Los Angeles on my own and do whatever I needed to do if I let him know. It was the first sign of my dad giving up a little of the control he always wanted to have over me. I continued taking a couple of classes over the summer, but they were fun classes. One was an acting class. I was around people with the same interest as I had, and the professor was a young theater actor who reminded me of the choir teacher on *Glee*. He was fun and flirty, and it was just what I needed to break away from the huge house I lived in with just my dad and his wife. It inspired me to continue pursuing my dreams of entertainment.

All the monologues I performed in class, I also put on my You-Tube channel, filmed in my dad's living room. I posted other videos more regularly on my YouTube as well. I was more inspired, more creative, and more tan. It was fun to have that outlet. When my real life wasn't all that exciting, my cyber life sure was. Driving up to LA was also my outlet, and maybe I didn't get to do every student film I wanted or go up for every last-minute commercial, but it still was sufficient.

And after a few months off, I wanted to get back into the comic con circuit. This time it wasn't about the money; it was about being around people and being around Mr. Eighties-Television-Sitcom-Cop-Star, as my sex life was nonexistent at my dad's house. I went to these conventions in my little costume, had my comic con boyfriend, and flew home back to reality. I think this messed with my head. If you have a side life, a sort of fantasy life, when you do head home to reality, you can get severely depressed. It's awful to have to go to class where no one acknowledges how awesome you are every time you walk into the room. I was so used to people wanting pictures with me and wanting to talk to me, I was sort of shell-shocked not to have anyone care who I was or what I was doing.

My relationship with my mom started getting stronger that year as well. She was going through some shaky times in her new marriage. I really only met Stepdad Number Three a couple of times—once at a comic con in Novi, Michigan, and once when they came out for my brother's college graduation. However, I always wanted to listen to my mom. I missed her, and I always genuinely felt we had the strongest mental connection to each other in my family. She understood my ways and the reasons I did the things I did. I don't think anyone else could ever grasp it. We talked on the phone a few times a week, and she and my sister sent me care packages. My sister, Kalli, came out more often to visit to get away from the situation back there, and we became much closer. We started becoming friends rather than just sisters who had to live together because we had the same mom.

I turned twenty, and I felt a little bit of anxiety that I was wasting my life in this town, going to college, living with my dad, and being isolated. I was itching to move back to LA after the summer, but I could never seem to save any money. I'd get checks from my dad, and I would go spend them on tanning or nails or some designer shoe. I just could not get my financials together, nor was I going to find anybody to rent to me because of my credit condition, so in a sense, I was stuck at my father's place. My father had gone through some financial struggles a few years prior due to bad investments, and that's when he started going to daily mass. He got up and went every morning, and he still does today.

In the fall, I went back to stripping secretly in City of Industry, which was about an hour away from my dad's house. I would say I was going to work at a funeral home overnight so it wouldn't seem weird I'd be coming home at four a.m. I hated lying to my dad, but I really wanted to make extra money to get out of the town where I was living and back to LA. I also wanted to quit school. Above anything else, I wanted attention again. I wanted to feel loved. When I performed onstage at these clubs, I felt like a star. Everyone wanted me. Everyone waited for me to get offstage so they could talk to me, dance with me. It made me feel fulfilled, made me feel beautiful. What didn't make me feel beautiful was the unwanted grabbing. Patrons were never supposed to touch us, but this strip club was paying us to be molested every night. I would cry on the way home, and I would stop by three or four fast-food chains to eat. I didn't gain weight because I was dancing eight hours a night, but food was my comfort as it had been when I was a child. It was something I could rely on, and it made me happy and calm. I'd get home, and my dad's office light would be on; he would wait up for me every night. I always saw this as a positive sign that my dad cared. He might've been overprotective, but he cared about me, and I had started to see this ever since my hospital incident.

I was feeling emotionally conflicted. Here my dad was paying me to go to school, allowing me to continue my dreams of acting, and waiting up for me, but all the while I was lying to him, stripping for money, getting molested every night for attention, and binge eating to no end. I talked to my dad about being depressed and confused about my direction and purpose in life, so he suggested I go to church with him, if I wanted. I started going with him every day. Even on the mornings I came home at four a.m., I'd wake up and go to church. Talk about a good-versus-evil struggle. I'd do something that was morally wrong and also mentally abusive to myself at night, and in the morning I'd pray for God's forgiveness. I was also praying for direction, the biggest constant prayer of my life. I am always struggling to find where I'm supposed to go in life. I really want to make God happy, and I also want to make myself happy. Why is this so hard for me?

I went to church every day or every other day and just prayed. I went to school during the day, and at night I watched TV with my dad until I had to go to work. On the weekends, my dad and I went to the movies and out to eat. It was nice to have a year with my dad in a relatively peaceful environment. It reminded me of the times in Illinois when my mom would take me out to the movies and shopping on the weekends. It was just quality time with family doing normal family activities. This will be the only time I use "normal" and "family" in the same sentence when it comes to myself.

Even though I loved living with my dad, I hated living with his wife. There are a lot of issues to discuss about her. I haven't even touched the tip of the iceberg when it comes to her in this book because I want this to be about my life, and I try to omit any memory or recollection of her being in it. She loved the power she had over my dad, knowing her investments with his money were the downfall of his career and financial control. When he went through financial troubles, the logical thing to do would have been to sell the big mansion the two of them lived in with no kids and move to a condo or something smaller. She never would. She would never even sign the papers so my dad could borrow money on the line of credit on his house that he bought from selling his business. It totally blows to be helpless. My dad would never divorce her because it's against the Catholic faith, and maybe because she would get half, or maybe he is fine with the situation. I admit, I judge him for staying with her.

Not only is she the one who caused most of the financial troubles by investing in her interior design dreams and real estate ambitions, but she was very manipulative when it came to me. It was very rare to go to the movies with my dad alone, and it was very rare to spend any time with my dad alone. As I'm writing this, I like to say my dad and I, even if in reality it's my dad and his wife and I. She was a tagalong for most everything, but I never acknowledged her then, and I don't now. Even with church, my dad went every day on his own for years prior to me moving back in, but when I started going with him, she started going with him. What a coincidence that when I moved out, and even today in 2013, my dad went to daily mass alone.

Any issues my dad brought up with me were because of her. I had to do chores. She thought I should have to help out around the house even though they paid for maids to come every other week. She thought that since I was working, I should pay rent. This was the "get out now" card I was waiting for—do not pass go, do not collect two hundred dollars, just get out now.

I prayed so hard to God to find a way for me to get out of my current living situation, to get away from her. I prayed for my dad's happiness, but I also prayed for my own and my own peace of mind. I looked for auditions anywhere and drove up to any of them, scraping for a sign to move back to LA and build up some money. I even considered moving in with Brian, who I kept in touch with through e-mail, just to get out. He wanted to get married. I didn't, but I was *this* close to doing it to escape the prison in which my dad's wife was the warden.

I booked a reality show pilot in January of 2009; it was all about day trading. To pick up slack on the lavish lifestyle my dad (i.e., my dad's wife) was used to living, my dad and my brother started a day trading company around 2007. They designed computer programs to day trade S&P future contracts. I only submitted because the grand prize was ten thousand dollars, and I knew I could fake my audition by saying words like "S&P future contracts." It worked. I booked it, and I went to stay in LA for four days to shoot the pilot.

A reality show pilot is quite different from being on a reality show; you generally won't get paid for it, and it won't usually air. It's usually shot to shop around to networks, and if it does get picked up, they may or may not recast you. Either way, I was excited to have a chance to win such a large lump sum and use it all for getting my butt back to Hollywood before I spent it all.

My dad gave me a crash course on day trading the week before I went to film. I sat with him for five days every morning from five a.m., California time, to about noon. We'd watch the commodities go up and down, and he'd tell me when to buy and when to sell, how to go long and stay short. I can't recall much now, but there were lots of calculations involved. He showed me where to put invisible lines to make it easy to know when to get out of a trade. I admire my dad for many reasons; he built his own company and made millions, and he is very smart. He figured out these strategies on his own, and I was always in awe of that. He made good money doing this, and I just always hoped I'd have his genes in the sense of being able to do the same. I consider myself an entrepreneur, even writing this book. I think I get that drive from my dad's side.

Filming the pilot was an intense four days. Everyone was on edge. We were all actors who knew a little about day trading. At twenty, I was going up against all these people who were in their late twenties all the way up to midforties. I doubt myself a lot in life, and this was no exception. I had just learned how to day trade the week before and was terrified. The first three days of filming we were on teams, and nobody wanted me on theirs. I was last picked and was the first eliminated in the challenge to win the first bonus one hundred dollars. It was some trivia-type setup, where they asked you questions about stocks and their symbols and other pointless things that even my dad didn't know, nor did he need to know when it came to trading.

I think everyone saw me, as usual, as the nonthreat. They saw me as being there for my looks and to be ditzy. I admit with this one I really didn't know a whole lot, or at least I didn't know as much as I said I did.

The third day we were in teams of three, and this was to eliminate people for real, to be out of the running for the grand prize. We were trading live on dummy accounts but with that day's market. It was one of the most exhilarating experiences I've had. I knew when my dad and I were trading we always made a huge profit. As a team of three, we each got an hour to trade. I was right in the middle of the day, and I did not like trading when I didn't get in at the beginning of the day, because I couldn't use information from the previous day's stock reports. We were trading stocks and not commodities, so it was a little different but the same concept.

My teammates, as well as the other team, were playing safe with their money. Trading a few stocks here, selling a few stocks there, probably playing with a total of fifty different stocks. It was a weird method, a strategy I knew nothing about, so I stuck with what my dad told me.

I remember everyone, including the creators and producers, was shocked by what I was doing. I can't remember this day's big events—all I remember is my teammates telling the cameras they were against something, but I did it anyway. By the end of my hour, we were tens of thousands of dollars ahead of the other team, when all of a sudden someone kicked our computer out, and it all was lost and shut down on our end. We were back at zero, and we were penalized for a technical error. It was devastating. Fortunately the last guy squeaked by the other team by mere dollars. We did win that round, and we had to face off against each other to see who would go into the final day. Everyone on my team got his or her own computer, and we had one final hour of trading to do; the two who made the most in that hour got to advance to the final round of the competition, which was trading an entire day, one on one.

In a weird turn of events, the only other girl competing and I advanced to the final two. It was bizarre, and I don't think anyone was expecting that. That morning of the final showdown, I consulted with my dad about the day before, and he gave me three big stocks that he would invest in for the day. I took those and ran with them. Right as soon as the stocks opened, I bought three hundred shares of Google for a ridiculous price and a few shares of eBay for safe measure, then just rode those out the entire day. When the end of the trading day came to a close, they had both of us go to the center of the stage, where the host was in true reality show form to announce the results. The host said, by a landslide, the winner of "insert title here" is…Trisha! I started crying, and then—what else?—I blacked out.

I remember them having the physical cash there and handing it to me, but that was it. I do remember getting in my car and shaking. I was shaking because I won. I was shaking because I had so much money. I was shaking because of what this meant for my future. I remember having to get gas on the way back to my dad's house and being paranoid about the money in my car when I was pumping. I just stared at it, and on the way home, I kept it in the passenger seat, just ten grand sitting in my purse in cash. I remember calling my dad to tell him, and the pride in his voice was something I had never heard before. We went out to dinner—his wife came too, of course—to celebrate.

There was a thought in my mind that perhaps I would use the money to get a boob job. My boobs have been uneven since I was twelve. I was always hoping that they'd even out over time, but they never did. At age twenty, my right breast was a D cup, and my left breast was a B cup. I had gotten use to stuffing and wearing two bras, but I really wanted to get an augmentation. Again, since I'm the world's worst saver, I didn't think I'd ever have the opportunity to afford the surgery. I contemplated getting that done instead of moving, but the sign I needed to decide came within a matter of weeks.

CHAPTER 9

HOLLYWOOD, HERE I COME...AGAIN

Valentine's Day came around, and my dad, his wife, and I were going out for dinner since I didn't really have any friends, nor did I have a boyfriend. We had done this the previous year, and it was nice not to be alone for the holiday. However, jealousy reared its ugly head with my stepmom, and she told my dad I was uninvited. They went out alone, and I remember bawling on the phone to my mom and sister that I felt so alone and abandoned, again, and that I needed to get out. My sister was already out of state at the time, on account of my mom getting married to a man in Michigan, so they had every right to move out to California if they wanted to. My mom's marriage wasn't making her happy, so she decided to get a divorce and move out to Los Angeles. One thing I will say about my mom and her marriages: I know she is mortified by how many times she's tied the knot and divorced, but I admire her for getting out of something that was making her miserable. I won't speak for my dad, but what I observe in his marriage is a lot of jealousy, unhappiness, and maliciousness. My dad's rules for divorce never included unhappiness, and I always asked him about this. His answers are fuzzy, but if something is tearing you down emotionally, isn't that a form of abuse?

The timing was perfect. I found all three of us an apartment in the Valley; it was a beautiful two bedroom, but I was willing to share a room with my mom if it meant getting out of the prison that was my dad's house. With my new winnings and my mom's tax return, we were able to split the deposit, get our credits approved, and move in. I continued to go to church, and this was the first time in a long time that I felt alive and optimistic. I was close to my auditions, and I was again with the family I had known growing up. We all got along so much better as adults. I was living off little acting jobs I got here and there. I worked consistently, doing background work, audience jobs, various talk shows, and reality shows. I searched all day on Craigslist and casting websites for any gig that paid. I even made up stories to get on certain shows. Lying is pretty much the same thing as acting, and I considered myself an actress.

I had booked one of my biggest roles to date, a lead in the Eminem video "We Made You" as the fat Jessica Simpson. Hollywood sure is relentless to celebrities who gain a few pounds, but nevertheless, it was tremendous exposure and a big paycheck for me at the time. I had my first viral video after the video was released. My "World's Fastest Talker" video had hit one million views in the first four months it was up, which was my record. I saw a little bit of money from YouTube for the first time. I had made a couple hundred dollars from that video, and that encouraged me to keep making more. It was quite remarkable that a video of me just speed-reading a passage from a book would acquire such an audience. I still don't fully understand the appeal of that video; as I'm writing this, it now has over six million views. Maybe because it's weird, maybe because people think it's fake or that it sounds like I'm speaking in tongues, or maybe it's because my giant padded bras made my boobs look like F cups. Either way, I felt like I was succeeding at something I've always wanted to make a living doing, which was entertaining people.

After the Eminem video, people started contacting me. No longer was I begging people to look at me or call me in for something. I mean, I still was, but I was getting more opportunities just for me and not competing with other girls. Plus-size clothing and lingerie companies contacted me for modeling opportunities. I was short, but I was curvy, and as I've been told my entire life, I carry my weight well, and my body proportions are pleasing to the eye. I got e-mails from companies that wanted me to model their clothes in catalogs, on billboards, online, etc. I even did a couple of romance novel covers. I loved modeling; it was easy work, and the fact that I was considered a plus model meant I could still eat and not have to starve myself. It helped pay the bills, which I actually did this time around thanks to my mom keeping me on track. I understood the value of a dollar, and I understood bills came first, and if that meant not having money left over to buy a new bag, I wasn't getting that new bag. Things were going pretty well by the time I turned twenty-one. I felt like I had control over my life.

In June of 2009, I experienced my first painful death. Both of my grandfathers had died when I was in junior high, but I wasn't super-close with either, so I didn't have a mourning period with their passing. However, one day as I was looking on MySpace to see if Brian had checked in, I noticed a blog posting that said he had passed away. I was shocked and confused, and I found out he had committed suicide, something he always said he was going to do before he turned fifty. In e-mail exchanges for the three years we knew each other, I knew he wanted a wife and children, but I also knew he wanted it to happen sooner rather than later. He had issues, but he never was as open with his as I was with mine.

I was devastated because of how we left things. The month before he died, I had asked him if he wanted to get back together, but I think after so many times of blowing him off and putting him on the back burner, he was sick of me. He told me to never contact him again and that he was "fuct" and I was "fuct." I asked him if he wanted to go see a concert with me in August of 2009, and he replied by saying he wasn't going to be around then. He had said this a lot—"if I'm around," "if I'm still alive then," etc.

It's not that I thought he was joking. I just didn't know what to do. He told me things when I was depressed, like, "Don't call suicide help lines because they will take you to a mental hospital." I guess it should've been a warning sign that he knew this. I just didn't know how to deal with someone who didn't want to live. He didn't speak to his family, and he didn't have close friends, so there was no one for him to talk to or reach out to about how he felt. The truth of the matter is that if someone really wants to take his own life, there is not much you can do. I tried to be there and be his friend and listen, but you can't control other people's actions.

His death hit me hard because he was someone who always was willing to help me out in every way, including financial. He was like the father I've always wanted, supporting my dreams and goals even if they were not his, and helping me out financially to achieve them. It was like I had lost my father, and it was a scary feeling because I felt like he abandoned me. In May when he said to not contact him again, I didn't take him seriously. He said that a lot when he was upset or hurt by me, but I was always able to pull him back in because of our connection. Not anymore—he was gone, but I didn't want to believe it. This was the beginning of my bad summers. The whole summer, I sat in my apartment, ate myself into a coma every night, and had no motivation to do anything. Life didn't seem real, life seemed unfair, and circumstances seemed to get worse.

Nobody in our household really had a job, so we were all on top of each other. My mom, of course, started going back to her old ways and talking to Stepdad Number Three again. My sister really lost her purpose out here. She didn't know what she wanted, and I think she missed her friends. I resented her again for little things, like having her own room when I had to share a bed with my mom. It irritated me, and so I started getting ready to run again as soon as I could. I lacked motivation to do YouTube videos, and nobody remembered me from years ago to help me get any sort of auditions. I found a strip club a few blocks away from my house. I went back in, and it felt like the only real home I'd ever had.

This strip club was a Valley strip club. If you go to a strip club in the Valley, you're going into a whorehouse, basically. My club was run by Persian men, and our managers were Mexican ladies. This was the club I thrived at the most because it was mainly full of minorities, both dancers and customers. I was the only white girl working at the club, which meant I was a rare gem.

The only time I had sex in the club with someone I didn't recognize, just an average citizen, was when I first started working in this club. I wasn't getting any dances, no girls were, and the only way he'd do VIP with me was if I agreed to have sex with him. It was awful, and I cried and ran out halfway through. He was semiattractive, which was the only reason I agreed, but I was having sex with someone I didn't want to for half of a VIP dance, which was a sixty-dollar payout. I was used to getting thousands of dollars from people in the entertainment industry who I would've had sex with regardless of the money just a couple of years prior.

I knew I was sinking back lower, but I couldn't really stop. I let people continue to do everything else. I felt worthless. I felt like this was my life, and I had to accept it. I've often been questioned by my family and a few boyfriends if I'm bipolar. The truth is that I'm not. I have sought out therapists and psychiatrists, and both just think I have experienced some traumatic events, but I'm not bipolar. If I ever felt bipolar, however, it was during this time. I would go to the club and just not care about STDs or really how I looked, and I would feel absolutely miserable, as if life wasn't worth living. The next day I'd go out to eat and shop, which are my two biggest endorphin rushes. So it really was two lives. At the same time, I was doing YouTube more regularly, just as a hobby, and I was talking about how happy I was when I knew, in just a few short hours, I'd be back at the strip club, which was basically a street corner.

In September 2009, one of my superhero friends from the show called and said she was going to be at a local comic con down in Long Beach, and she wanted to know if I'd share her booth with her. I was excited because it was something to get me out of the house, and it wasn't a strip club. I didn't go in my traditional Limelight costume that Sci-Fi had given me, but I went in the traditional Limelight colors—Limelight 2.0, as I liked to call her. The first day of the three-day convention was a Friday. I went in one of my silver stripper skirts and a silver sequined bra with lime-green fishnet over top. I felt good. I felt sexy. I felt like a stripper walking the comic con floor.

I was on a break and walking around the con just looking at everything and taking pictures for my blog when one of the actors on celebrity row stopped me. "Honey, hey honey, come over here," he said. I knew his name but wasn't sure who he was. He was standing up with his other cast mates from a TV show he had just done, and I thought he was so handsome. I looked down at his pictures he was selling, and he looked so different as a kid, compared to the man who was standing in front of me. As a kid he had made movies in which he always played a geek, sort of the awkward, scrawny type with braces. I wasn't familiar with any of his films or the TV show he had completed a couple of years prior, so I wasn't really starstruck, but I was in awe of his looks and his charm. We chatted for a few minutes, but then I had to leave to get back to my own booth.

Within an hour, his assistant or friend came over and gave me a card with this actor's name and number. For the sake of this book and his privacy, we'll call him Mr. Perfect. Mr. Perfect was about six feet one inch, with broad shoulders, blond hair, blond eyelashes, and the prettiest blue eyes you'll ever see. He had huge hands, which I noticed right away, and a manly and fresh scent to him that I dreamed about. He was the first guy who I was giddy to go see, to go out with. I envisioned our marriage and babies that first night after meeting him. His friend asked me for my number to give to him, so I did. Let's get real. I was never going to call him first. I would never have the confidence. I didn't see him for the rest of that day, but I had butterflies all that night and couldn't sleep.

I was up at three a.m. the next day to go back to the convention. I wore a silver sequined dress this time with lime-green gloves. I got there right before the convention opened to set up my booth, and he was about an hour late after the show started. I saw him come in, and he came immediately over to the booth where my superhero girlfriend and I were signing, and he gave me a kiss on the cheek and a hug and called me beautiful. He said we should hang out soon and that he'd call me. I was floating. I just was gushing. The other superhero gal with me was about fifteen years older than I was, so she was excited because she knew who he was, which in turn made me feel even more special that he knew who I was and wanted to go out with me.

I left the con early that day because it was slow, and I didn't say good-bye to him because I was too shy to talk to him. As I was driving home, I received a phone call; it was him. I was so nervous that I couldn't even speak. Mr. Perfect wanted to go out that night down in Long Beach, but I was already in traffic headed back to LA. He then suggested we blow off day three of the con and that I go to his beach house. I said yes, no questions asked.

Mr. Perfect's house was beautiful, right on the ocean in a little beach town. I was terrified. I had on a Forever 21 sundress and wedges. He greeted me with a really long kiss on the lips. I was taken aback. No guy had ever been this forward when we hadn't even been out on a date yet, and we hadn't even really had the "getting to know you" chat. The kiss led to making out, which led to his bedroom. From past experience I knew how this was going to end, but I was so attracted to him that I didn't care. I didn't care that he might give me money for this or he just might never call me again. I wanted him so badly, and I was down. He didn't wear a condom, but I didn't care. I wanted to have his babies the first day I met him. We had the best sex I've ever had, even to this day. It was beautiful, and he held me afterward. I had never been cuddled before this point; isn't that crazy? I always either left immediately afterward, or I would just lie there in a cold slumber.

We then got up and showered together, and he said he'd take me out to breakfast. *What?* He wanted to spend time with me even after we had sex? This was unheard of to me. I was so giddy. We sat next to each other on the same side of the booth, and he ordered for us. I couldn't even eat, I was so nervous. He was Prince Charming; he was my Mr. Perfect, and the fact that he drove a black Porsche didn't hurt either. He paid for us, and we went back to his house, had more sex, and talked and walked on the beach and watched movies. We spent the whole day together. I had to leave that night to go in to work because Sundays were the only days I was making money, and I knew I couldn't fall behind on my bills, especially now that my mom and sister were living out here, and we were all surviving paycheck to paycheck, so to speak.

I remember telling him what I did and that I had to leave, and he was really sad. He asked me if I'd come back after work, and I said, "I don't know. It's so late." I remember him getting really upset because apparently earlier in the day, he'd asked me to stay another night with him and forever, and I guess I said yes, but that was during lovemaking. I'd say anything to him. I wasn't thinking straight. I said I'd call him after I was done and see how tired I was. We were hot and heavy really fast. He told me he loved me that day, and I told him I loved him. Is this normal? Absolutely not. However, I knew we had this connection, and it was a connection in the worst kind of way.

CHAPTER 10

THE ONLY MAN I'VE EVER LOVED

I really was in love with Mr. Perfect right away. He had success, beautiful possessions, good looks, and lots of wisdom to share with me. He made me feel safe. He talked about marriage and babies the first months we were together, and I wanted that so badly. Over time it wasn't even about him having money; in fact, I told him I'd sign a prenup because I didn't want any of his money if it meant us being together forever. I was living a fairy-tale life. Yes, I still stripped a couple of nights a week when I had to, and I did what I had to do to make sure I made money while I was there, but the rest of my life was spent at Mr. Perfect's beach house. We'd go swimming, he'd take me to fancy dinners in Beverly Hills, we'd have amazing sex, and we'd cuddle and talk; that was our life. We would spend five days together and never leave the house.

He also introduced me to the world of the dominant/submissive relationship. I had no idea there was a whole subculture for this at the time, but I thought it was hot. I'd call him "Daddy" and "Master," and he referred to me as his "little girl," and I loved it. He was the father I'd always wanted, but unlike Brian, I was deeply attracted to him and everything he did. He was my daddy, and he was going to take care of me forever.

This love affair only lasted a few months, until one day I saw him on a gossip site while he was on a "business trip" in NYC, where his girlfriend had called the cops on him for banging on her door and harassing her. I was devastated. I called him in hysterics, and he tried to tell me none of it was true. I was like, "Do you have another girlfriend? Why wouldn't you tell me? Why would you have unprotected sex with me if you're doing this with everyone else?" He used the fact that I was a stripper against me, and I hung up the phone on him. I sent him a million nasty text messages throughout that weekend about how old he was, what a loser he was, and that he was a has-been and washed up. He just never returned my texts or calls after all that. I constantly googled him every day to see what he was up to. He had gotten a bit part on a sitcom, and then I saw paparazzi pictures of him and a different girl in NYC kissing at a hockey game, and that was the punch in the gut I needed to move on.

I went back to stripping, but I also looked into escorting more. I found an ad on Craigslist for an agency that I went to work for. I also looked on sugar daddy sites on the Internet. I was looking for love and acceptance, but I was also looking for guys to take advantage of, even though they would think they were taking advantage of me. I got these guys to fall in love with me, and then just changed my number and never talked to them again. *There! How do you like being abandoned?*

In January 2010, I spoke to my old neighbor Superman again about possibly getting on *Jimmy Kimmel Live*. We did a segment on the street in costume one day together, and he introduced me to some writers who were interested in my speed talking and possibly breaking a world record on the show. I never went through on *Jimmy Kimmel Live*, but that was the push I needed to get back into auditioning. I did a string of reality shows here and there, and it felt like I was relevant in the world of entertainment again. When we shot the segment for *JKL*, one of Superman's friends—we'll call him Alvin—came by and offered to take us to lunch. Superman whispered in my ear that this guy was a millionaire and would pay us just to have lunch with him.

Alvin eventually started taking me out alone for lunch and shopping. He'd buy me whatever I wanted, and at the end of the day, he'd give me a thousand dollars cash. We never had sex, nor did we even kiss. To be honest, he was repulsive to me. He made my stomach turn. He was a nice friend in the beginning. I felt bad that he had nobody and that he looked forward to the days we spent together. We went to dance clubs where people just made fun of him. He was that guy. That guy who thought he was cool and hip when in reality he was an overweight sixty-year-old man who wore a toupee and white overalls with no shirt and no rhythm. We lasted about six months until he started becoming possessive. He'd show me his gun collection and tell me how nobody would be able to hear the guns go off with a muffle he had. Eventually he caught wind that I went out to eat with Superman and not him, and that's when he flew off the handle. He left threatening messages and harassed me. I told my mom about it, and she called him; apparently that was enough to scare him, and he stopped. I changed my number and moved on and stuck with pure sex and stripping for money.

The summer of 2010 was equally as depressing as the summer before, if not worse. I missed Mr. Perfect, and he showed up on movies of the week and shows all the time. I tracked him on sites where photographers sold images from Hollywood events, and I always saw him with a different girl. I was a glutton for punishment. I booked no television jobs, the strip club was so slow, and my escort agency had closed. I got really sick as well and found out I had contracted a few minor STDs. No STD is minor in my eyes, but at least I was able to control and get rid of the ones I had. It was scary to have such a wake-up call. I knew I had to stop escorting and not do anything with anyone at the strip clubs except dance.

Work picked up in the fall, and I focused on my YouTube videos to generate income so I could stop dancing altogether. I was only making a few hundred dollars a month with my online videos, so it wasn't enough to stop completely, but it was enough to cut back my time at the club.

I started dating a customer at the club named Amir. Amir was from Tehran, Iran, and was a Muslim. He had a very thick accent and spoke Farsi at the bar with the owner of our club. The owner always had a liking for me because he thought I looked like a Barbie—that and I made a ton of money for him. Amir never got dances from anyone, and he would just sit there to pass time. He was in LA for ten months on business; he had a construction company and was working on a building. The owner introduced us, and we had a genuine connection.

I always was good at showing interest in customers, but I really had an interest in Amir. He was really different but really generous. He used to pay me just for my time to talk to him, and he'd get a few dances here and there with me and tip me an absurd amount. The money was a huge attraction, but he was young as well. I believe he was thirty-three, and he was about six feet four inches. We saw each other outside the club for dinner and drinks, and he paid me, but eventually I told him that he didn't have to do that. He'd still come into the club to tip me hundreds of dollars while I was onstage, but we did start dating without the money each date. It was nice, and it felt real, but I didn't see myself with him for the long term. It was a nice distraction to date someone again and not think about Mr. Perfect.

Amir eventually had to go home at the beginning of 2011, and we stayed in touch. He said maybe one day we'd get married and have kids and that he'd be back for me. We talked for a few months until the summer of that year. Before the summer started, I found him as a friend suggestion on Facebook and saw that he had already been married for the past ten years. Another man, another lie, another marriage Trish got in the middle of.

Well, it was summer again, which meant I was due for another bout of depression. Our lease was up, and my mom and sister wanted to move somewhere cheaper. I wanted to be out on my own, so they found another two bedroom, and I was going to stay in our current apartment by myself. Within weeks, the police raided the club for solicitation, and it was shut down. My mom and sister were gracious enough to let me move in with them, but it meant sharing a bed and a bedroom with my mom yet again, for another year.

CHAPTER 11

THE YEAR OF YOUTUBE

After another summer of me sitting on my butt doing nothing productive, I tried to find a hobby I could do every day to occupy my time and my mind. I started putting out YouTube videos every day. I put out videos on everything from how I was feeling, to what I was wearing, to sketch comedy, and more. People were responding to my daily videos, and I started to double in views on a weekly basis. As I got more followers, I was inspired to do more and put more out. I loved the feedback I got from people who watched my videos. I saw that I was helping a lot of people and entertaining them. It was so fun to have people come back every day to watch me and see what was happening in the life of Trish.

I was able to support myself just barely by making videos and doing my TV jobs whenever I could. My peace of mind came back, and I really felt like I was doing something with my life and actually helping others. I focused on acting jobs and got more exposure. I got calls from TV shows after they saw my business e-mail on a video. I got called to be on a few talk shows with my fast-talking talent, and it was a wonderful chain of events. I'd put a YouTube video up, and producers would see it and find me and put me on their show, and in turn people would see me on the show and come and find me on YouTube. The popularity really kept escalating, and I loved it. I was performing, and even though I wasn't rich, I was able to keep my dignity, keep clothes on, and still earn money. I also got my first sponsorship in 2011. Someone was actually going to pay me to test out and talk about their product in my video. I was on cloud nine. I thought I had really made it.

In September 2011, almost two years after I had met Mr. Perfect, he resurfaced in the news for being arrested for disturbing the peace in his neighborhood. Seeing him on all these gossip sites again made all those passionate memories come rushing back. I still had his e-mail and decided to reach out to him just to see if he was OK. I can't recall exactly what I said, but it was something along the lines of, "You may not remember me, we dated briefly, but I just wanted to make sure you were OK," and I signed it *Trish*. He e-mailed me back the next day to my surprise and said thank you, and he said he was out of town focusing on his writing and that he'd be back in town that weekend if I wanted to get together. I was beside myself with excitement. He sent an e-mail the Saturday morning he got back. He explained he wasn't dating anyone, and if I wasn't, we should go out for breakfast. I called him back right away and said yes and to save my new number. He texted me about a half hour before I was going to leave, saying how excited he was to see "this," and he texted me a picture that wasn't me. I was crushed. This rollercoaster that Mr. Perfect put me on was fast.

I texted back and said, "Um, that's not me. Let's do a rain check for today." He apologized and said he thought it was another Trish, and he begged me not to reschedule. He asked for a picture to help him remember. I will say this: Mr. Perfect is a big pothead. He smokes a lot of marijuana, and his memory is not great. At times he'd ask where his keys were when he was holding them, or he couldn't remember a movie we had seen the day before. I wanted to see him again, and secretly, I wanted to have sex with him again. I sent a picture. I said I would come under the conditions that we were meeting only as friends and that he'd have to tell me where we met first, so I would know he really knew who I was.

He got it exactly right, which helped my bruised ego a little bit. I didn't care; we had breakfast and went back to his beautiful beach house. He started to kiss me and get on me. I tried to resist and play hard to get. I stopped him and said we should catch up or talk first. That didn't last long; we were right back to what I had remembered: lots of passion and lovemaking, and it was wonderful. Sex is wonderful when it is with the right person. As we started back together again, it was even kinkier than I remembered. He had dog collars and leashes and whips, and I loved all of it. He was so dominating, and that's what I liked. I liked to make him jealous because it showed he cared. As I'm writing this in early 2013, I still have his voice mail on my phone from the day after we reconnected. It's his deep and sexy voice. "Hey, baby, I'm so happy you came back to me. I love you." I gushed at the table with my mom. She noticed how much happier I was.

Mr. Perfect really pulled out the stops this time around. He took me to Newport Beach within the first week of us being back together. It was amazing. He even wanted to meet my mom and sister. This was a sign that he was serious to me. He occasionally went to NYC for a few days at a time to visit family. I kept an open mind. I told myself I would be OK if he was seeing someone else, and that I wasn't going to flip out if I found out he was dating another girl.

I didn't want to snoop, but I did. We were friends on Facebook, and he only had about thirty people on there, including his mom and his sister. I looked on sites to see if he was seen anywhere with anyone. He continued to do comic cons, and I saw him with his arms around girls in those cities. I was hurt; after all, that's how he wooed me at a comic con. He asked me to come with him on occasion, but I did have to keep generating income with little jobs here and there. One day I read on a message board that he was seen at a restaurant with his girlfriend in Boston. It kind of hurt, but I pushed it aside because I didn't want him to cut off communication with me again.

He was always great about texting. He'd text me a dozen times a day; it was so nice to be thought of. He'd come back to LA, I'd pick him up at the airport, and all was right in the world again.

I contracted some more STDs from him, and when I confronted him about it, he apologized and offered money for my medications and doctors' visits. Yet I still continued dating him. I was upset because I was no longer stripping or escorting, and I was only having sex with him, but I still caught some stuff. I asked him if he could just tell me if he was sleeping with other girls so I knew to use a condom with him. He never told me, but I knew. I knew because I saw that other girls had logged into Facebook from his computer, and their e-mails were still there, but I never had to see them, and he still spent the majority of his free time with me. I guess if I wasn't available, he had backups.

He still was Mr. Perfect because he still talked about marriage and babies. I knew he cared for me, and he shared his whole life with me. He told me all about his problems from childhood to now, really intimate details that I couldn't imagine him sharing with every floozy. He had a lot of issues with his mother and I think trust issues in general. I could relate. To this day, I don't trust any men, not one. I sabotage relationships before they even start because I know in my head it'll end in heartache. I don't blame him for his womanizing ways. I blame myself for not thinking I deserved better. In my heart, I wanted him to change, but I knew he wouldn't.

I was desperate to keep him. When I had saved enough money, I finally got my breast augmentation and lift in January 2012. If anything solidified his love and care for me, it was my recovery. Mr. Perfect stayed with me in my bed every night and catered to me every day. He bought me magazines and food, and we watched TV. He had to go shoot a TV show for a week in Canada, and that week he was gone was when I experienced complications with my surgery. I had gotten an infection from sweat going into my stitches. This was the second time in my life that I thought I was going to die for sure. I got chills, and I couldn't breathe. Every day that passed I felt like I was being buried alive, like my lungs were closing. My surgeon gave me antibiotics and demanded an immediate checkup. He changed the wrapping, and I felt better, but he told me to take it easy.

When Mr. Perfect came back it was close to Valentine's Day, and I really wasn't supposed to be out and about, but I didn't want to lose him. When he asked if I'd go on a business trip with him to Palm Springs, I said yes. I couldn't even bathe myself or lift my arms to do my hair, but I agreed. We hadn't had sex in about a month, so on the trip we had pretty vanilla sex, which I shouldn't have been doing, and sure enough the stitches in my right boob popped open. We drove back on Valentine's Day, and Mr. Perfect took me to my surgeon's office in Beverly Hills. I had to go and get another surgery the next day to take out a little bit of the implant and get stitched back up. Mr. Perfect drove me to my surgery early in the morning, and he took me back to his house. He got me my medications and took the best care of me. I felt like he really loved me. He was OK not having sex with me either, when I said I was scared of popping my fresh stitches. To me, this was what made him different. I don't know; the relationship wasn't healthy with the cheating and lying, but I loved him. It's true what they say: the heart wants what the heart wants.

At the tail end of my recovery, Mr. Perfect got a big acting role in a movie produced by a major studio, and he had to go shoot in Romania for a month. I was so happy for him because I knew he was struggling with his life in Hollywood and his position as an actor, whether he was relevant, blacklisted, a joke, etc. It was a great script with a great cast. I had to stay back to get my stitches out, but a week after he got over there, he asked for me to come over and be with him. I had planned on doing just that, especially since he was going to be over there alone for his birthday, but I had to postpone it due to my call for *America's Got Talent*. *America's Got Talent* had contacted me via my YouTube channel for many seasons to do my fast talking as a talent. Knowing I would get booed for doing that live on national TV, I had declined many times, until Howard Stern was announced as a judge. When they contacted me yet again to come on the show, I agreed. Mr. Perfect had actually driven me to the first audition for producers earlier that year. I told him I would come over after my audition in Austin, Texas.

On the night before my audition, I checked Mr. Perfect's Facebook page. A girl who had commented "I love you" before on his page wrote something along the lines of how amazing it had been to see him before he left and to hurry back to her. It was the last straw for me. I couldn't keep doing this to myself. I bawled my eyes out and just thought of how awful I must be that he had to cheat on me. She wasn't pretty—she was plain—but it still was a dagger to my heart. When he called me that night before my audition, I asked him point-blank if he saw this girl, and he said yes. I broke down. He tried to calm me down and said that he hadn't slept with her, but she had messaged me saying that she had. He met her after we got back together, and that was the most painful part. I wasn't good enough for him. I wasn't ever going to be. He was a liar, like me, and he just didn't care about me the way I did about him. I told him to never contact me again.

The next day I went to audition for the judges on *America's Got Talent* after hysterical tears and angry e-mails to Mr. Perfect the night before. I pulled it together and got my character, Trish, ready. I was there to meet Howard and get people to notice me, and I did. From the first moment of being backstage, to stepping on the stage, to dancing with Howard, to the moment I got in the van to go to the airport to go home, I blacked out the whole experience. When my family asked me how it went, what had I said to Howard, what had I done, I said, "I don't know," because I really didn't know. I was terrified to see it air because I had no recollection of doing or saying any of the things that I did. It turned out to be harmless, and it got me a lot bigger audience on my YouTube channel, and of course, I got to meet another one of my idols. See, I told you I have a knack for meeting the people I want to meet; it'll happen one way or another.

YouTube was there for me as a form of therapy to occupy my mind and time. It also allowed me to start saving. I'd never saved money in my life, but I made it a point to put away half of my paychecks from YouTube just to be smart.

I did continue to talk to Mr. Perfect. I apologized for lashing out at him, and he apologized as well. I could feel us drifting, but I enjoyed doing video chats with him while he was on set in costume. His life and work intrigued me, and I just enjoyed being a part of it. When he came home, we took things slowly. It wasn't as passionate as before. I saw him for my twenty-fourth birthday, and we had sex, and that was about it. He got busy, and I sort of just stopped pushing it. He didn't love me, and he didn't even say it anymore.

I felt myself getting crazy on him. I made random lies about going to get married in Boston and a bunch of other things that made no sense. I didn't like that I had to lie to him to get his attention or to keep him in my life. I was even confusing myself with all the lies. I started reading the other girls' Facebook posts as well, and eventually I just let him go. He did the same. I tried to start fights to get him to talk to me. I think the last one was about a sweater I left at his house, and if he didn't send it back to me, I was going to get a police escort to come and get it. That was probably it for him as well. I really had lost my mind at that point. What I was doing was nothing a sane person would do. This was early June, the summer, and I was preparing for the season of depression.

I decided to seek help—professional help. I took some of the money I was earning from YouTube and started to see a therapist. The therapist referred me to a psychiatrist, and after a few months he referred me back to a therapist. I justified spending the money on something that seemed silly to me by taking the advice I was getting from therapy and sharing it with my YouTube audience, a win-win for everyone.

Therapy helped a lot with every aspect of my life. It was an unbiased listener who told me my feelings were OK, that crying was OK. Throughout my childhood and teen and adult years, everyone dismissed my feelings. I was always told I was overdramatic, I lied too much, I wasn't worth listening to, and my emotions were out of control. It was validating to hear another human being—three, actually—say my emotions are totally justified.

I have a lot of issues to deal with. I'm still dealing with them. My therapists helped me realize what my relationships were about in the past and how to make them better in the future. Between therapy and church, I realized I was worth more than I gave myself credit for. That God has forgiven me for my sins, but now it's time to forgive myself.

I moved out of my mom and sister's apartment into my own beach house at the end of the summer, and I felt happy. I felt like I truly had broken my summer depression cycle by seeking help. After moving out, my relationship with my mom and sister strengthened. We see each other a few times a week and talk every day, while each of us still has her space. I talk to my father almost every day, and we just talk about the now and not about the past. My brother is still my rock in life. He's always there to listen. He has found a great job and a great fiancée, and I'm so happy for his happily ever after.

Me? Well, I'm still waiting for mine. Living on my own and on the beach is a dream come true. My backyard is the ocean. I have a walk-in closet and a princess-style living room fully furnished with a bed and everything. I'm sitting on my big couch watching the sun set and drinking a glass of wine from my bar. The past six months or so of living on my own have brought clarity to my head. I no longer have to depend on anyone. I'm secure in my finances and in my career. I'm always looking to better myself, but as of now, I'm happy. My YouTube is booming, and people are being entertained. Love me or hate me, you're watching me and giving me attention; it's what I like, but not what I need.

CHAPTER 12

TO BE CONTINUED...

Who's ready for the sequel? I know I am, except God has not written it yet. I'm sorry, but there's no fairy-tale ending for this book. I wish I could say I'm exactly where I want to be. I don't think I'm quite there, but I will say I'm having fun on this journey called life. I am at peace with my family, and after this book, I can finally let go of the past. I don't dwell on the past because I can't change it. I can only focus on the present because that's what I'm living. My relationship status is single, but the most important relationship I've ever had, my relationship with Christ, is stronger than ever. I'm still in therapy but not as often. I am receiving help for my food addiction and shopping addiction. I've abstained from sex for the past eight months to wait for the right guy. I am proud of what I have accomplished on my own, and I see my worth, and my body will be a gift to someone who is worthy, not someone who is paying me or someone who is passionate. I'm no longer seeking love, but if love finds me, I will not be afraid.

I am slowly learning to trust people again. Even if someone has broken my trust, I will not hold that against the next person who comes into my life. I'm working on being a bit more extroverted as well. I'm currently in an improv class, and it's one of the most fun things I've done in my life. I'm expanding the brand that is Trish with my online clothing boutique, in which I work with my dad, and my very own perfume will be out this year. Oh, and hey! Did I mention I'm writing another book?

No longer am I plagued by self-doubt. Your dreams are actually easy to achieve. I've always wanted to write a book, and now I've written a book. I wanted to make a career out of entertaining people, and now I am. I can no longer go out in public without at least three young girls coming up to me and saying how excited they are to see me in person, and that they watch me on YouTube every day. It tickles my heart, and if all this were to go away tomorrow, the fact that I got to experience such love and attention is plenty for me.

I don't know how you feel after reading this book, but after writing it, I feel inspired. Perhaps it has come off as bitter at points, and maybe it's depressing, or maybe you're sickened by things I've done. I'm sure some people are convinced I've lost my mind, but I honestly look back and think, "Trish, you've made yourself happy in your own life, and that's what's important." My family is healthy, and so am I. I can't ask for any more. I do pray that you all find your happiness as well. Life really is a journey. Try not to worry so much about where you end up; just enjoy what is happening now, and enjoy the people you're with. Please yourself first and foremost, and do what makes you happy. Take chances and keep the faith. Life is short, life is hard, but life is also beautiful. You woke up today with air in your lungs, so you know you are here on this earth for a reason. You have purpose, and you are loved. Go out and inspire, go out and live, and go out and love.

Thank you all who are reading this from the bottom of my heart. You've made one of my biggest dreams come true: being a published writer. Thank you for letting me entertain you, and thank you for caring about me for these past few hours or days, or however long it took you to read this. I love you for that. This was quite a trip down memory lane, and I'm so excited to share the next part of my life with you all. Stay tuned...to be continued...

Made in the USA
Middletown, DE
29 November 2020